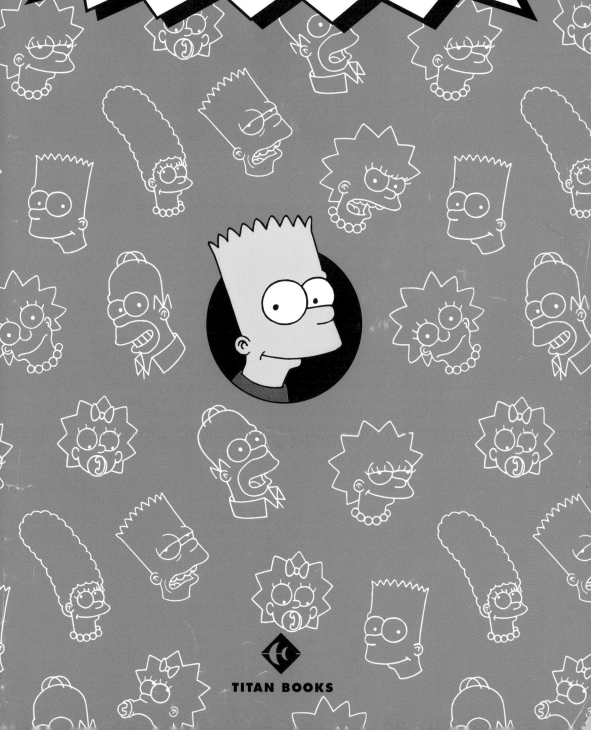

SIMPSONS™
COMICS EXTRAVAGANZA

Titan BOOKS

Dedicated to the memory of Snowball I:
Though you are gone, your claw marks
on our comic books remain.

SIMPSONS COMICS EXTRAVAGANZA. Copyright ©1994 by
Bongo Entertainment, Inc. All rights reserved. Printed in Canada.
For information address Bongo Comics Group c/o Titan Books.

Published in the UK by Titan Books Ltd., 42–44 Dolben Street,
London SE1 0UP, under licence from Bongo Entertainment, Inc.

FIRST EDITION: OCTOBER 1994

ISBN 1 85286 597 0

8 10 9

Publisher: MATT GROENING
Editors in Chief/Creative Directors: STEVE VANCE, CINDY VANCE
Managing Editor: JASON GRODE
Art Director: BILL MORRISON
Contributing Artists: TIM BAVINGTON,
PHIL ORTIZ, SONDRA ROY
Contributing Writers: DEB LACUSTA, DAN CASTELLANETA
Book Design: MARILYN FRANDSEN, DEBORAH ROSS
Publicity Director: ANTONIA COFFMAN
Legal Guardian: SUSAN GRODE
Printed in Italy

CONTENTS

WELCOME TO SIMPSONS COMICS EXTRAVAGANZA, MAN!

Over the several years that the Simpsons have been cavorting on TV (since 1987, if you count the prehistoric shorts on the "Tracey Ullman Show"), we've gotten the kinds of compliments that cartoonists crave hearing: you're setting a bad example, you're corrupting youth, you're frightening Americans about nuclear power, you're hastening the downfall of western civilization. But my favorite prissy outrage at Simpsonian subversion came in 1990, when school principals, busybodies, and petty government officials across the land flipped out because of the Bart Simpson underachiever T-shirts—you know the ones, with Bart saying "And proud of it, man!"

The point of that T-shirt was that no kids call themselves underachievers—that's a label middle-achieving grown-ups slap on mischief-achieving kids. And the proper wisenheimer response to being labeled an underachiever, of course, is to be "proud of it, man!" Of course, none of the Simpsons critics gave us any credit when we followed up the Bart Simpson Underachiever T-shirt with a Lisa Simpson Overachiever T-shirt. But that may be because on that T-shirt we had Lisa saying, "Damn I'm good!"

Which brings me to the Simpsons Comics Extravaganza. This consists of the remarkable first four issues of Simpsons Comics, brought to you by the Bongo Comics Group, a small but overachieving band of merry artists, designers, lawyers, and publicists, namely: Steve Vance, Cindy Vance, Bill Morrison, Jason Grode, Susan Grode, and Antonia Coffman. Their work looks effortless, but believe me, the Bongo gang has shed several droplets of sweat, a few driplets of blood, and perhaps even a couple tears of joy in the making of these comics. Don't worry, however: All Bongo bodily secretions have been wiped off the original art so as not to distract you from your entertainment experience.

As Bart might say, We're proud of these comics, man. As Lisa might say, Damn, they're good.

And as Marge might say, I don't want you sitting up in that treehouse all day reading comic books! You'll ruin your eyes!

MATT GROENING
Bongo Comics Group

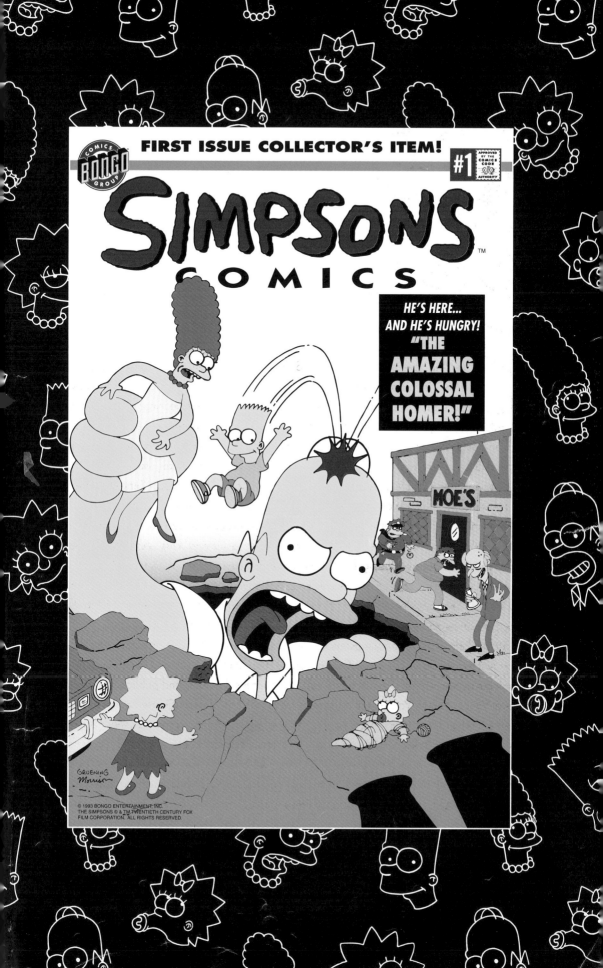

BART'S BOTTOM 40

1. LISA'S SAXOPHONE
2. VEGETABLES THAT DON'T FLY WELL OFF YOUR SPOON
3. WRINKLED OLD GROWNUPS - - I HOPE I NEVER BECOME ONE
4. THE CHEAP LOUSY PRIZES THEY GIVE AWAY IN BOXES OF FROSTY KRUSTY FLAKES
5. HAVING NIGHTMARES THAT I'M A CHIP OFF THE OLD BLOCK
6. BEING CAUGHT RED-HANDED
7. THE HARDENED CRUST ON THE TOP OF MOM'S CASSEROLES
8. THE GOOEY STUFF UNDERNEATH THE HARDENED CRUST ON THE TOP OF MOM'S CASSEROLES
9. PRINCIPAL SKINNER'S SPECIAL FILE ON ME
10. THE "NO DRAWING ON THE WALL" RULE
11. THE FACT THAT OTTO HARDLY EVER LETS ME DRIVE THE SCHOOL BUS
12. CREAMED CORN
13. PARENTS WHO HAVE SIGNATURES THAT ARE REALLY HARD TO FORGE
14. ACCIDENTALLY FEELING GUM STUCK UNDERNEATH A RESTAURANT TABLE
15. SUCKING ON YOUR PEN IN SCHOOL AND HAVING YOUR MOUTH FILL UP WITH INK
16. NAMBY-PAMBY G-RATED MOVIES
17. DAD'S SNORING THAT YOU CAN HEAR THROUGH THE WALL EVEN WITH A PILLOW COVERING YOUR HEAD
18. STORIES WITH MORALS AT THE END
19. CARTOONS WITH NO FUN VIOLENCE AND PAIN
20. CARTOONS WHERE THEY RUN PAST THE SAME LAMP AND TABLE A ZILLION TIMES
21. THE STRAWBERRY AND VANILLA PARTS OF NEOPOLITAN ICE CREAM
22. GAS STATION RESTROOMS
23. MAKING BAD WORDS WITH MY ALPHABET SOUP AND HAVING LISA TELL ME THEY'RE MISSPELLED
24. ACCIDENTALLY DRINKING OUT OF THE GLASS WHERE GRANDPA KEEPS HIS FALSE TEETH
25. THE DIFFICULTY OF LOADING WATER BALLOONS WITH MAPLE SYRUP
26. SUGARLESS ANYTHING
27. BEING TRIED IN COURT AS AN ADULT
28. VENGEFUL BARBERS
29. THE HAUNTING THOUGHT THAT SIDESHOW BOB WILL GET OUT OF JAIL AGAIN
30. RIP-OFF CHOCOLATE BUNNIES THAT ARE HOLLOW INSIDE
31. COMIC BOOKS WITH INSUFFICIENTLY GIMMICKY COVER ENHANCEMENTS
32. PHLEGM (ALSO ON MY TOP 40 LIST)
33. WHEN MOM SAYS "IF ALL YOUR FRIENDS JUMPED OFF THE BRIDGE, WOULD YOU JUMP TOO?"
34. CARTOONS WITH REDEEMING SOCIAL MESSAGES
35. THE NONEDIBLE DECORATIONS ON BIRTHDAY CAKES THAT YOU ACCIDENTALLY TRY TO EAT
36. BRUSSELS SPROUTS
37. FORGETTING ABOUT THE CANDY BAR YOU PUT IN YOUR PANTS POCKET ON A REALLY HOT DAY
38. SWIMMING POOL BELLY-FLOPS THAT BOTH HURT AND LOOK DUMB
39. THE BOTTOMS OF YOUR SNEAKERS AFTER YOU COME OUT OF A PETTING ZOO
40. BEING AN "UNDERACHIEVER" - - TO TELL YOU THE TRUTH, I'M NOT EXACTLY SURE WHAT THE WORD MEANS

WHOA! *263 POUNDS* -- A *NEW RECORD!* WAY TO GO, HOMER!

D'OH!

HERE'S SOME NICE FLUFFY TOWELS RIGHT OUT OF THE DRYER -- BART, WHAT ARE YOU DOING?

I'M READING THE SCALE FOR HOMER. HE CAN'T SEE PAST HIS BELLY.

OH, HOMEY, YOU'VE BEEN *SNACKING AGAIN!* I ASKED YOU NOT TO EAT THOSE COOKIES IN THE COOKIE JAR.

I'M SORRY, MARGE -- BUT I JUST COULDN'T RESIST THOSE LITTLE BOW TIES WITH THE PINK FROSTING ON TOP.

THEY WEREN'T *BOW TIES*, THEY WERE *HOURGLASSES.* I BAKED THEM FOR PATTY AND SELMA'S *BIOLOGICAL CLOCKWATCHERS ANONYMOUS* MEETING TONIGHT.

ULP!

LATER...

REMEMBER, NOW, ONLY *ONE DONUT* TODAY!

I PROMISE... :SNIFF:

ONLY ONE DONUT-- IT'S NOT *FAIR!*

C'MON, MAN! GET A GRIP ON YOURSELF! YOU CAN DO IT. THE TRICK IS NOT TO THINK ABOUT DONUTS!

BUT EVERYTHING REMINDS ME OF DONUTS. THAT CLOUD EVEN *LOOKS LIKE* A GREAT BIG DONUT!

AND *THAT* CLOUD LOOKS LIKE A *BUNCH* OF GREAT BIG DONUTS!

D'OH

EAT US HOMER

MEANWHILE, AT THE NUCLEAR POWER PLANT...

UNNNHH!

SMITHERS

YOU BELLOWED, SIR?

DEAL WITH THIS BLASTED ANNOYANCE!

AND NEXT TIME, GET THE EASY-OPENING KIND!

UH, THIS *IS* THE EASY-OPENING KIND, SIR.

ZIP!

NEW E-Z OPEN!

14 KT GOLD PAPER CLIPS

AH, SMITHERS -- IF ONLY I POSSESED YOUR LITHE, YOUTHFUL ATHLETICISM.

PERHAPS THE PACKAGE WAS DEFECTIVE, SIR.

I'LL GLADLY FIRE OFF A *SCATHING LETTER* TO THE MANUFACTURER -- OR BETTER STILL, YOUR ATTORNEYS COULD *SUE THEM INTO BANKRUPTCY.*

THANK YOU, OLD FRIEND, BUT I'M AFRAID IT WOULD TAKE MORE THAN THE CASUAL RUINATION OF SOME INSIGNIFICANT OFFICE-SUPPLY MANUFACTURER TO LIFT ME OUT OF MY DOLDRUMS.

YOU KNOW, I WAS A RATHER VIRILE SPECIMEN IN MY DAY -- IN FACT, I ONCE BESTED THE MIGHTY *"MAN-MOUNTAIN" MACKENZIE* HIMSELF AT A GAME OF *QUOITS.*

≥SIGH≤ BUT LOOK AT ME *NOW,* SMITHERS --

-- ALL THOSE YEARS, AND WHAT HAVE I TO SHOW FOR IT? A BODY BETRAYED BY TIME.

AND A PERSONAL FORTUNE VALUED AT $2.6 BILLION DOLLARS.

THAT TOO, THAT TOO! BUT MERE WEALTH, NO MATTER HOW OBSCENELY OSTENTATIOUS, IS NO SUBSTITUTE FOR PHYSICAL WELL-BEING. AS LONG AS I AM BOUND BY THE CHAINS OF MORTALITY, WHAT FREEDOM CAN THERE BE IN RICHES?

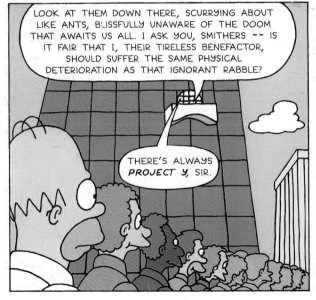

LOOK AT THEM DOWN THERE, SCURRYING ABOUT LIKE ANTS, BLISSFULLY UNAWARE OF THE DOOM THAT AWAITS US ALL. I ASK YOU, SMITHERS -- IS IT FAIR THAT I, THEIR TIRELESS BENEFACTOR, SHOULD SUFFER THE SAME PHYSICAL DETERIORATION AS THAT IGNORANT RABBLE?

THERE'S ALWAYS *PROJECT Y,* SIR.

BUT OF COURSE! *PROJECT Y!*

COME, SMITHERS -- WHAT SAY WE DROP IN ON THE BOYS IN R & D?

SOON, IN A SECRET ELEVATOR FAR UNDERGROUND...

PROJECT Y -- MY **YOUTH RAY**. WHY, JUST SAYING THE **NAME** SENDS A SUBLIME THRILL COURSING THROUGH MY VEINS.

IT CERTAINLY COULD BE A BOON TO HUMANITY, SIR.

BOON, SHMOON. DO YOU THINK I'VE POURED MILLIONS OF DOLLARS INTO THIS PROJECT SO THAT **JOE SIX-PACK** CAN HAVE AN EXTRA 50 YEARS TO WASTE SITTING ON HIS KEISTER READING **COMIC BOOKS**?

I DID IT FOR **ME**, SO THAT I MIGHT REGAIN THE VIGOR OF MY LOST YOUTH. THEN I'LL GIVE HUMANITY THE HELPING HAND IT DESERVES -- **THE IRON FIST!**

AH, DR. OLBERMAN. HOW GOES THE RESEARCH?

CONSTRUCTION IS COMPLETE, SIR! BEHOLD --

-- **THE REJUVENATOR RAY!**

IT STIMULATES HORMONE PRODUCTION, INCREASING THE GROWTH OF NEW CELLS. THIS SHOULD ACTUALLY **REVERSE THE AGING PROCESS**. ALL THAT REMAINS IS THE HUMAN TESTING.

TESTING? **NONSENSE!** WHAT AM I, THE **FOOD AND DRUG ADMINISTRATION**? BEGIN MY TREATMENTS AT **ONCE!**

UH -- REMEMBER **PROJECT Q**, SIR.

HMMM...

VERY WELL, PROCEED WITH THE TESTING.

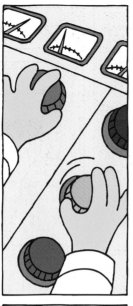

THE NEXT MORNING...

UNNH!

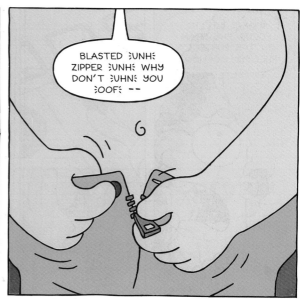

BLASTED ⌐UNH⌐ ZIPPER ⌐UNH⌐ WHY DON'T ⌐UHN⌐ YOU ⌐OOF⌐ --

FOR HEAVEN'S SAKE, ARE YOU ALL RIGHT? THE WAY YOU WERE GRUNTING, I THOUGHT YOU WERE HAVING A *HEART ATTACK!*

I'M FINE, MARGE -- BUT THESE PANTS MUST'VE *SHRUNK* IN THE WASH.

THOSE PANTS ARE *BRAND NEW* -- I HAVEN'T EVEN WASHED THEM YET. AND THEY'RE BIGGER THAN YOUR OLD ONES. HOW MANY DONUTS DID YOU EAT YESTERDAY?

AW, I ONLY --

RRRRIIPP!

⌐SIGH⌐ I GUESS I'LL JUST HAVE TO GO BUY THE NEXT SIZE UP. YOU HAVE TO HAVE SOMETHING TO WEAR TO WORK.

SOON...

HOMEY! I'M BACK WITH YOUR NEW PANTS!

HIGH & WIDE

HOMER?

OH MY LORD...

SUCK
SUCK

AND THIS JUST IN -- WE'VE ALL HEARD OF CHILDREN WHO GET TOO BIG FOR THEIR BRITCHES -- BUT APPARENTLY IT CAN HAPPEN TO *GROWN-UPS* AS WELL.

GOOD MORNING SPRINGFIELD

A MRS. MARGE SIMPSON RETURNED FROM BUYING HER HUSBAND A NEW PAIR OF PANTS ONLY TO FIND THAT HE HAD OUTGROWN THE *HOUSE*, TOO.

SKYCOPTER 6 - LIVE

THE STILL-GROWING MR. SIMPSON WAS LAST SEEN HEADING FOR DOWNTOWN SPRINGFIELD.

SPRINGFIELD INSURANCE COMPANY

IF YOU *EVER* SELL ANOTHER POLICY TO THOSE SIMPSON WACKOS, YOU'RE *FIRED!*

SAID MRS. SIMPSON, "THANK HEAVENS FOR HIS SUPER-STRETCH UNDERWEAR."

DID YOU HEAR THAT, SMITHERS? HE'S BECOME A *COLOSSUS!* WHY, THAT'S EVEN *BETTER* THAN BEING *YOUNG!*

BURNSLAND

IMAGINE! CHARLES MONTGOMERY BURNS -- STANDING ASTRIDE THE GLOBE! THEY'LL NAME *COUNTRIES* AFTER ME! I'LL BE LIKE THE JOLLY GREEN GIANT, ONLY NOT *GREEN,* AND *NOT JOLLY!*

LATER..

THERE'S YOUR FATHER NOW, MAGGIE. MAYBE HE THINKS HE'S ON HIS WAY TO WORK.

HOMER! HOMER, IT'S ME -- MARGE! HOMER, PLEASE STOP!

HONK!

HOMER

IT'S NO USE. I GUESS HE'S JUST SO BIG HE CAN'T HEAR ME.

IF ONLY THERE WAS SOMETHING WE COULD DO! AT THAT SIZE HE MIGHT ACCIDENTALLY HURT SOMEONE!

OOOOH

KONK

UUNNH

YAAAAAH!

ZZZIK

OH, HOMEY..

"MEANWHILE, THIS STORY, LIKE ITS SUBJECT, JUST KEEPS GETTING BIGGER, AS JOURNALISTS FROM AROUND THE WORLD POUR INTO SPRINGFIELD..."

WOW! THESE *HALLUCINATIONS* ARE GETTING MORE *REALISTIC* EVERY DAY.

LOOKA THE *SIZE* OF THAT GUY! I BETTER LAY IN AN EXTRA CASE OF DUFF!

ALAS, FRIEND HOMER, YOU HAVE ALWAYS BEEN MY BIGGEST CUSTOMER, BUT IT IS POSSIBLE TO HAVE TOO MUCH OF A GOOD THING.

LATER, AT SPRINGFIELD ELEMENTARY...

THIS DARN HEADACHE! I SWEAR I CAN ACTUALLY *HEAR* MY TEMPLES THROBBING.

THOOM THOOM

THOOM

≧GASP!≦

BART, I APOLOGIZE. YOU MAY GO NOW.

I WILL NOT EXAGGERATE MY FATHER'S WEIGHT PROBLEM
I WILL NOT EXAGGERATE MY FATHER'S WEIGHT PROBLEM
I WILL NOT EXAGGERATE MY FATHER'S WEIGHT PROBLEM
I WILL NOT EXAGGERATE MY FATHER'S WEIGHT PROBLE

NEARBY..

MAN, I NEEDED THIS BREAK. FULL POLICE MOBILIZATION IS *TOUGH!*

HOUSE-O-DONUTS

I'LL SAY. WE'VE BEEN ROLLING NONSTOP SINCE THE ORDER CAME DOWN. IT'S BEEN A HELLUVA 45 MINUTES.

THOOM

I HAVEN'T SEEN A SIGN OF THIS GUY. IF YOU ASK ME, THERE'S NO SUCH THING AS A GIANT MA--

THOOM

CRUNCH!

AAAIIIEEE!!!

...CHIEF WIGGUM EXPRESSED REGRET THAT HIS MEN WERE UNABLE TO **STOP** THE GIANT CREATURE, BUT COMMENDED THEM FOR THEIR CLEVER CHOICE OF A **STAKEOUT SITE**.

A GIANT STALKS SPRINGFIELD - DAY 1

JOINING ME NOW ARE TWO OF SPRINGFIELD'S LEADING HEALTH CARE EXPERTS, *DR. JULIUS HIBBERT* AND *DR. MARVIN MONROE*.

HIYA, KENT

DR. HIBBERT, FROM THE MEDICAL PERSPECTIVE, WHAT CAN YOU TELL US ABOUT THIS CASE?

WELL, KENT, AS THE SIMPSONS' FAMILY PHYSICIAN I'VE SEEN MANY UNUSUAL THINGS, BUT FRANKLY, THIS ONE TAKES THE CAKE.

:CHUCKLE:

DR. JULIUS HIBBERT

TAKES THE *FRUITCAKE*, YOU MEAN! AS I EXPLAIN IN MY NEW BOOK, "*I'M OKAY, YOU'RE SICK AND TWISTED*," THIS SORT OF PHENOMENON IS ROOTED IN WHAT JUNG REFERS TO AS THE COLLECTIVE UNCONSCIOUS!

THIS IS JUST A TYPE OF **MASS HYSTERIA**, FANNED BY THE SPECULATIVE RAMBLINGS OF ATTENTION-GRABBING, KNOW-NOTHING, SELF-APPOINTED **PSEUDO-EXPERTS**!

DR. MARVIN MONROE

HMMM, YES, WELL...

LET'S GO LIVE NOW TO THE HOME OF THE MAN WE'VE DUBBED "THE AMAZING COLOSSAL HOMER," AND SEE IF WE CAN HAVE A WORD WITH HIS UNFORTUNATE FAMILY.

WE'D PREFER NOT TO PARTICIPATE IN THIS MEDIA CIRCUS. PLEASE LEAVE US ALONE WITH SOME SHRED OF OUR DIGNITY INTACT!

EYE ON SPRINGFIELD - LIVE

SLAM!

WAY TO GO, LISA!

WHY, THANK YOU, BART. FRANKLY, I WOULD HAVE EXPECTED YOU TO SIDE WITH THE VULTURES WHO ARE TRYING TO CASH IN ON OUR MISFORTUNE.

WELL, UH...

HI, KIDS. I'M HOME.

MOM! ARE YOU OKAY?

I'M *EXHAUSTED!* I'VE BEEN CHASING YOUR FATHER ALL OVER TOWN. I FINALLY LOST HIM WHEN I RAN OUT OF GAS.

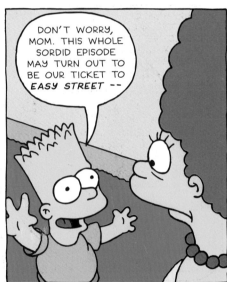

DON'T WORRY, MOM. THIS WHOLE SORDID EPISODE MAY TURN OUT TO BE OUR TICKET TO *EASY STREET* --

-- AND HERE'S THE MAN WHO CAN *PUNCH* THAT TICKET.

HI THERE. I'M LIONEL HUTZ, ATTORNEY AT LAW.

MY CARD.

"NEGOTIATING MEDIA RIGHTS TO PERSONAL TRAGEDIES MY SPECIALTY"?

THAT'S RIGHT, MRS. SIMPSON. I CAN HAVE YOU ON THE HOLLYWOOD GRAVY TRAIN FASTER THAN YOU CAN SAY *"MOVIE OF THE WEEK!"*

I'M SORRY, MR. HUTZ, BUT I'LL HAVE TO ASK YOU TO LEAVE MY HOUSE *RIGHT NOW!*

KIDS, GET IN THE CAR -- WE'RE GOING TO SEE THE MAYOR.

SOON, IN A TOP-SECRET COMMAND CENTER BENEATH CITY HALL...

THE AFTERNOON POLLS ARE IN, SIR. YOU'RE DOWN 11% BECAUSE OF THIS GIANT GUY.

SOUNDS LIKE THE TIME IS RIGHT FOR A BIT OF *JINGOISTIC MILITARY ADVENTURISM.* WHAT'S THE POOP, WIGGUM?

WE'VE GOT ALL OUR SQUAD CARS ON THE STREET -- EXCEPT THE 12 IN YOUR PERSONAL MOTORCADE, OF COURSE. WE'VE BEEN TRACKING *JUMBO BOY'S* MOVEMENTS FOR THE PAST HOUR.

CUT THE SMALL TALK, WIGGUM. WHAT'S THE BOTTOM LINE?

HE'S HEADING FOR THE *NUCLEAR POWER PLANT.*

YOU MEAN...

YEAH. IF HE CRASHES THAT PLACE, IT'S *GOODBYE SPRINGFIELD,* HELLO *SLOW AGONIZING DEATH BY RADIATION POISONING!*

LET ME IN!

WHAT TH--?!

I'M MRS. HOMER SIMPSON, AND I *DEMAND* TO SEE THE MAYOR!

IT'S OKAY, BOYS -- LET HER GO.

QUIMBY, ARE YOU OUTTA YOUR MIND? YOU CAN'T LET A CIVILIAN IN HERE! SHE'LL SEE *EVERYTHING!* SHE'LL SEE *THE BIG BOARD!*

SHUT UP, WIGGUM. THAT'S A *REGISTERED VOTER* YOU'RE TALKING ABOUT.

NOW WHAT CAN I DO FOR YOU, MRS. SIMPSON?

I WANT TO KNOW WHAT YOU'RE GOING TO DO FOR MY HUSBAND, MR. MAYOR.

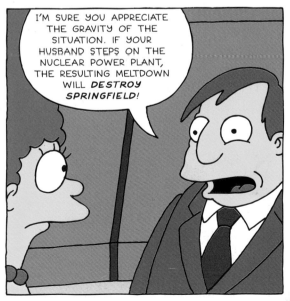

I'M SURE YOU APPRECIATE THE GRAVITY OF THE SITUATION. IF YOUR HUSBAND STEPS ON THE NUCLEAR POWER PLANT, THE RESULTING MELTDOWN WILL *DESTROY SPRINGFIELD!*

THEREFORE, IN THE BEST TRADITION OF OLD HOLLYWOOD MONSTER MOVIES, I'VE CALLED THE *PENTAGON* TO ARRANGE AN *AIR STRIKE* AGAINST YOUR HUSBAND.

WHAT?!

AN *AIR STRIKE!* COOL!

YOU CAN'T DO THAT! HOMER COULD BE *KILLED!*

NOW, MRS. SIMPSON -- I'M NOT SAYING THAT HE WON'T GET HIS HAIR MUSSED, BUT IT'S MY DUTY TO PROTECT THE PROPERTY OWNERS OF OUR FAIR CITY.

BESIDES, MAYBE THIS'LL CONVINCE A FEW OF THOSE *BASE-CLOSING PEACENIKS* BACK IN WASHINGTON OF THE STRATEGIC IMPORTANCE OF THE *SPRINGFIELD AIR FORCE BASE.*

ETERNAL VIGILANCE AGAINST GIANT MONSTERS IS THE PRICE OF LIBERTY.

PERHAPS I MIGHT SUGGEST AN ALTERNATIVE...

MR. BURNS! I'M ALWAYS HAPPY TO HEAR THE VIEWS OF OUR TOWN'S LEADING PLUTOCRAT.

FOR MY OWN,, UH, *HUMANITARIAN* REASONS, I WANT THIS CREATURE BROUGHT IN *ALIVE.* I BELIEVE WE'VE FOUND A WAY. DR. OLBERMAN?

WE HAVE DEVELOPED A DRUG WHICH WILL RENDER THIS GIANT UNCONSCIOUS AND RETURN HIM TO HIS NORMAL SIZE. THERE IS, HOWEVER, ONE DRAWBACK --

WE HAVE ONLY BEEN ABLE TO MANUFACTURE ENOUGH OF THE SERUM FOR A SINGLE DOSE. WE WILL GET BUT *ONE SHOT* -- AND WE *MUST NOT MISS.*

ONLY ONE CHANCE, EH? SOUNDS TOO RISKY TO ME.

I HAVE AN IDEA!

HEH HEH! ISN'T THAT CUTE! YOU JUST SPEAK RIGHT UP, LITTLE LADY!

SINCE TIME IS OF THE ESSENCE, I'LL OVERLOOK YOUR CONDESCENDING ATTITUDE.

I KNOW HOW YOU CAN BE SURE OF GETTING A CLEAR SHOT AT HIM. ALL YOU HAVE TO DO IS...

MINUTES LATER, AFTER A QUICK BRIEFING...

ALL RIGHT, PEOPLE, YOU KNOW WHAT TO DO. LET'S GO *BAG THIS BIG GUY!*

OKAY, BOYS -- LOOK SHARP! *HERE HE COMES!*

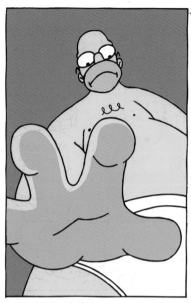

FIRE!

THOOF!

THUP!

KATHUMPH

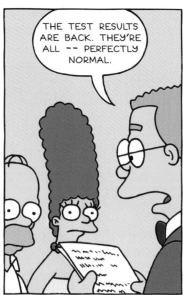

GREETINGS, ALL YOU COAGULATING COMICS FANS! IT'S YOUR BLOOD-CURDLING BUDDY *BART SIMPSON* HERE, WITH A TRAUMATIZING LITTLE TALE THAT'S GUARANTEED TO GIVE YOU A *FOUR-COLOR FRIGHT.* DO YOU GET A THRILL OUT OF TRACKING DOWN A NEAR-MINT TREASURE? DOES YOUR HAPPY LITTLE HEART PALPITATE WITH PLEASURE WHEN YOU PURCHASE A RARE BACK ISSUE? WELL, YOU MAY WANT TO *RECONSIDER* AFTER YOU READ THIS! I CALL IT...

THE COLLECTOR!

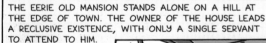

| A MATT GROENING PRODUCTION | STEVE VANCE SCRIPT & LAYOUTS | SONDRA ROY PENCILS | BILL MORRISON INKS | CINDY VANCE COLORS | SUSAN GRODE INSPIRATION |

THE EERIE OLD MANSION STANDS ALONE ON A HILL AT THE EDGE OF TOWN. THE OWNER OF THE HOUSE LEADS A RECLUSIVE EXISTENCE, WITH ONLY A SINGLE SERVANT TO ATTEND TO HIM.

LITTLE IS KNOWN ABOUT THE OWNER, FOR HE IS GRUMPY AND ANTI-SOCIAL AND SHUNS CONTACT WITH THE TOWNSFOLK BELOW. RUMOR HAS IT, HOWEVER, THAT HE IS FABULOUSLY WEALTHY, AND THAT HIDDEN DEEP IN THIS HOUSE IS A TREASURE BEYOND IMAGINING.

INSIDE THE GREAT HOUSE, THE SAME ROUTINE IS OBSERVED EVERY EVENING. AFTER GORGING HIMSELF ON AN ENORMOUS MEAL OF GOURMET DELICACIES, THE OWNER RETIRES TO THE COMFORT OF HIS FAVORITE CHAIR. WITH HIS FAITHFUL DOG AT HIS FEET, HE SAVORS A FINE CIGAR AND AN AFTER-DINNER DRINK.

THE PORK CHOPS WERE SLIGHTLY OVERCOOKED, SMEDLEY. DO IT AGAIN AND YOU'RE FIRED.

VERY GOOD, SIR.

THEN COMES THE HIGHLIGHT OF HIS EVENING -- IN FACT, THE ONLY PART OF HIS ENTIRE EXISTENCE THAT GIVES HIM ANY TRUE PLEASURE -- AS HE SETTLES IN TO READ A SELECTION FROM HIS ENORMOUS LIBRARY -- A LIBRARY PAINSTAKINGLY ASSEMBLED AT UNSPEAKABLE EXPENSE THROUGH YEARS OF OBSESSIVE COLLECTING -- *THE WORLD'S GREATEST LIBRARY OF COMIC BOOKS!*

AH, *CAPTAIN SQUID* #7 -- WITH THE FIRST APPEARANCE OF HIS SIDEKICK, *LI'L SQUIDDIE!* HOW WELL I REMEMBER THE DAY I BOUGHT THIS BOOK.

"THE OWNER OF THE LOCAL COMICS SHOP REFUSED TO NEGOTIATE ON THE PRICE -- UNTIL I THREATENED TO TELL THE VICE SQUAD THAT HE WAS SELLING BETTY PAGE TRADING CARDS TO MINORS. WE SETTLED ON 10% OF GUIDE. I LEFT THE SHOP CLUTCHING MY LATEST PRIZE -- ONLY TO BE ACCOSTED BY SOME LOWLIFE LOITERING OUTSIDE."

'SCUSE ME -- DO YOU HAVE A LIGHT?

"I TAUGHT THE RUFFIAN A SHARP LESSON."

YAAAH! KEEP AWAY FROM MY PRECIOUS MINT COPY!

"OF COURSE, AFTER THAT DISTASTEFUL INCIDENT, I'LL NEVER PATRONIZE THAT STORE AGAIN."

LATER, HIS READING DONE, THE COLLECTOR COMPLETES HIS EVENING RITUAL. HE CAREFULLY RETURNS THE PRECIOUS COMIC TO ITS PROTECTIVE SLEEVE...

...THEN HE CARRIES HIS TREASURE DOWN AN ANCIENT STAIRCASE TO HIS CELLAR.

THERE, AMIDST BOXES AND CRATES OF LONG-FORGOTTEN HEIRLOOMS, HE HAS CONSTRUCTED A HOME FOR HIS COLLECTION...

THE LADDER CRASHES TO THE FLOOR AND THE FRIGHTENED DOG RACES OUT OF THE VAULT, BRUSHING AGAINST A PRECARIOUSLY BALANCED STACK OF CRATES...

THE CRATES TOPPLE AGAINST THE VAULT DOOR, AND IT SLAMS SHUT -- *LOCKED!*

INSIDE THE VAULT, THE COLLECTOR COOLLY ASSESSES HIS SITUATION...

YAAAH! I'M TRAPPED!

WAIT -- CALM DOWN -- DON'T *PANIC!* THERE'S GOT TO BE A WAY OUT SOMEHOW. *THINK*, MAN -- WHAT WOULD *RADIOACTIVE MAN* DO IN THIS SITUATION?

I KNOW! HE'D CRUMPLE THE DOOR WITH A SINGLE *ATOMIC-POWERED PUNCH!*

THE COLLECTOR IMMEDIATELY PUTS HIS PLAN INTO ACTION -- BUT TO NO AVAIL!

UNNNHH!! CRUMPLE, BLAST YOU!

WELL, WHADDYA KNOW -- I GUESS MAYBE USING BRUTE STRENGTH TO RESOLVE PROBLEMS DOESN'T ALWAYS WORK AS WELL IN REAL LIFE AS IT DOES IN COMICS.

LOOKS LIKE I'M STUCK HERE UNTIL SMEDLEY COMES HOME AND LETS ME OUT. OH WELL, I GUESS I'LL JUST HAVE TO SPEND MY WHOLE WEEKEND READING COMICS -- WHAT A SHAME! HEH HEH!

CUT OUT FIGURES (OR BETTER YET, USE A PHOTOCOPY!) AND PASTE ON LIGHTWEIGHT CARDBOARD. TO STAND, FOLD BASE AT A AND B.

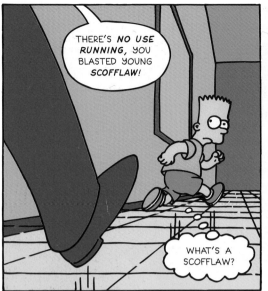

I'VE HAD **ENOUGH** OF YOUR SHENANIGANS, SIMPSON. SINCE DETENTION IS CLEARLY AN **INSUFFICIENT DETERRENT**, THIS TIME WE'LL TRY SOMETHING NEW! A PUNISHMENT SO **HARSH**, SO **BRUTAL** -- SO --

WHAT'RE YOU **TALKING ABOUT**, MAN?

SOMETHING SO **AWFUL** I--I HAVEN'T EVEN **THOUGHT OF IT YET!**

BE IN MY OFFICE AFTER SCHOOL.

YOU TOO, VAN HOUTEN.

BUT **WHY ME**?! I DIDN'T **DO** ANYTHING!

LET THIS BE A LESSON TO YOU, YOUNG MAN -- WE'RE JUDGED BY THE COMPANY WE KEEP.

BESIDES, ARBITRARY PUNISHMENT IS A PREROGATIVE OF POWER.

SOON, IN SKINNER'S OFFICE...

THE **PRINCIPALS' CONVENTION** IS JUST WEEKS AWAY! IF I CAN KEEP THE LID ON AROUND HERE 'TIL THEN, I'VE GOT A SHOT AT BEING NAMED **DISCIPLINARIAN OF THE YEAR!**

I'VE GOT TO **CRACK DOWN** ON THESE REPEAT OFFENDERS, -- BUT HOW?

PERHAPS I'LL ASK MOTHER...

ACH!

IN THE MEANTIME, WILLIE, HOW'S OUR **BELOVED MASCOT**?

NOTHIN' A BIT O' ELBOW GREASE AN' SOME **SPIT** WON'T TAKE CARE --

THAT'S IT!

WILLIE, IN YOUR OWN RUSTIC WAY, YOU'VE HIT ON THE **ANSWER!** MAKE ROOM IN THE TROPHY CASE -- THAT AWARD IS IN THE BAG!

NAY, SIR! YE **CANNA MEAN** --

YES! I'M SENDING THOSE BOYS TO --

"SCARED SPITLESS!"

AND SO, THE NEXT DAY...

HEY, WAIT A MINUTE! THIS ISN'T THE *FIREWORKS FACTORY*!

VERY OBSERVANT, NELSON! YES, I'M AFRAID THAT PROMISE OF *FREE M-80'S* WAS JUST A RUSE TO GET YOU BOYS TO COME ALONG QUIETLY!

SPRINGFIELD STATE PRISON

WELCOME FUTURE OFFENDERS

YOU'RE HERE TO PARTICIPATE IN THE TOUGHEST *ANTI-DELINQUENCY* PROGRAM KNOWN TO MAN! IT'S CALLED *"SCARED SPITLESS!"*

BUT WHEN DO WE GET OUR *FREE M-80'S?*

AH -- CHIEF WIGGUM! WHY DON'T YOU TELL THE LADS ABOUT THE *DREADFUL, TERRIFYING THINGS* WE'LL BE SEEING TODAY?

MY PLEASURE, SEYMOUR.

WE HAVE A SAYING IN LAW ENFORCEMENT, BOYS: "A *FRIGHTENED* CITIZEN IS A *LAW-ABIDING* CITIZEN."

THE REASON FOR THIS LITTLE CONFAB IS TO SHOW YOU THE *HORRORS* OF PRISON LIFE -- TO *SCARE* YOU SO BAD THAT YOU'LL DO *ANYTHING* TO BE SURE YOU NEVER COME BACK!

YOU'LL *NEVER TAKE ME ALIVE*, COPPERS! I'VE *SEEN* THE INSIDE OF A CELL -- I'D RATHER *DIE* THAN *DO TIME!*

WOW!

OUR GOAL IS TO CHANGE YOU FROM THE *MINDLESSLY REBELLIOUS KIDS* OF TODAY INTO THE *MINDLESSLY OBEDIENT ADULTS* OF TOMORROW!

YOU KNOW, CHIEF, I MIGHT WANT TO INCORPORATE PART OF THIS PROGRAM INTO OUR GENERAL CURRICULUM.

WHILE YOU'RE HERE, YOU'LL EXPERIENCE ALL THE DEGRADATIONS OF INCARCERATION. YOU'LL DRESS LIKE CONVICTS AND YOU'LL BE TREATED LIKE CONVICTS. HERE, PUT THESE ON.

COOL -- REAL PRISON CLOTHES!

THIS IS IT, BOYS -- THE HARSH REALITY OF PRISON LIFE. IT'S A WORLD OF LOCKED DOORS, BARRED WINDOWS, AND UNCOMFORTABLE PLASTIC CHAIRS.

AND NOW, THE MOMENT YOU'VE ALL BEEN WAITING FOR -- YOUR OPPORTUNITY TO COME FACE-TO-FACE WITH A *REAL, LIVE CRIMINAL!*

THIS IS #354708, BETTER KNOWN TO HIS BUDDIES HERE AS *SNAKE*. WE'LL LEAVE YOU BOYS IN HIS CAPABLE HANDS.

SEE YOU LATER, CHIEF. I'D LIKE TO THANK YOU FOR PROVIDING ME THIS CHANCE TO KEEP THESE KIDS FROM MAKING THE *SAME MISTAKES* I DID.

C'MON, SEYMOUR, LET'S HIT THE GUARDS' LOUNGE BEFORE ALL THE CRULLERS ARE GONE!

SOON...

...AND ANOTHER THING -- IF YOU'RE STEALING A *GETAWAY CAR,* BE SURE IT HAS *GAS* IN THE TANK.

WOW! THIS IS THE MOST *EDUCATIONAL* EXPERIENCE OF MY *LIFE!*

LATER...

...SO IN CONCLUSION, WHATEVER YOU DO, DON'T GET CAUGHT. THE FOOD HERE IS *LOUSY* AND THE *TV RECEPTION* IS *WORSE!*

WE ONLY GET *TWO CHANNELS* -- AND ONE OF THEM IS *FOX!*

ANY QUESTIONS?

YEAH -- WHERE'D YOU GET YOUR TATTOOS?

I GOT THIS ONE FOR CHRISTMAS. I STOLE A SPOON FROM THE CAFETERIA AND MADE INK FROM --

THAT'S ENOUGH, SNAKE --

--THEY'RE NOT SUPPOSED TO LEARN THAT STUFF TILL THEY'VE BEEN HERE A COUPLE OF YEARS!

NOW SHAKE A LEG, BOYS -- IT'S TIME FOR *LOCKDOWN!*

OUR PROCEDURE HERE, AT LEAST UNTIL THE NEXT AMNESTY INTERNATIONAL INSPECTION, IS TO THROW YOU BOYS IN A FILTHY JAIL CELL OVERNIGHT! YOU'RE GONNA SEE WHAT IT'S *REALLY* LIKE HERE.

TAKE 'EM *AWAY!*

HEY, LOOK, EVERYBODY! NEW SHORT GUYS!

GET IN THERE, PUNKS.

HEY, BAD BOYS!

WELCOME TO STIR, FOUR EYES!

OH, THE BITTER IRONY! A HACKSAW, THE INSTRUMENT OF MY DELIVERANCE, IS ALMOST WITHIN MY GRASP -- BUT MY *WOULD-BE CAPTORS* ARE HERE AS WELL!

THIS WILL REQUIRE A CERTAIN DEGREE OF STEALTH. REMOVE YOUR WORK SHIRT.

I'LL JUST DISPOSE OF THESE AND --

Toss

WHAT'S THIS?

A *HAT* OF SOME KIND! FATE INDEED SMILES UPON ME. THAT'S CERTAINLY A USEFUL ACCOUTREMENT --

OH, NO! ¡SHUDDER!¡

I MUST WEAR IT TO CONCEAL MY HAIR -- BUT YOU'LL *PAY DEARLY* FOR THIS *INDIGNITY,* BART SIMPSON!

A *DONUT SHOP!* THEN THE POLICE *AREN'T* HERE ON MY ACCOUNT! THE CAR IS EMPTY -- THE COAST IS CLEAR.

U GO NUTS 4 Donuts

STUFF STUFF

I ♥ KRUSTY

COME ALONG, MY SOON-TO-BE-*EX*-COMPANION!

SOON, INSIDE THE HARDWARE STORE...

AH, YES! GOOD HEFT -- WELL-BALANCED -- A FINELY-HONED BLADE --

A WORTHY TOOL TO FREE MYSELF FROM YOU --

-- PERMANENTLY!

MAN, HE'S REALLY GONE OFF THE DEEP END! I GOTTA GET AWAY FROM THIS MANIAC -- BUT HOW?!

HEY, MAC -- HELP ME OUT, OKAY?

I NEED TO BORROW ONE OF THOSE THINGIES TO OPEN A CAR DOOR. WE LOCKED OUR KEYS IN THE PATROL CAR, AND THAT SIREN'LL RUN DOWN THE BATTERY IF WE DON'T HURRY.

I'LL GO GET IT, CHIEF, BUT THAT'S THE THIRD TIME THIS WEEK. IF IT HAPPENS AGAIN, THE BOSS SAYS I HAVE TO CHARGE YOU.

STAY QUIET, BART, UNLESS YOU WISH TO HASTEN YOUR DEMISE.

HOLD IT *RIGHT THERE*, PAL.

WHY, HELLO, OFFICER -- WHAT CAN I DO FOR YOU?

I'M PUTTING THE WORD OUT TO ALL LAW-ABIDING CITIZENS -- WE JUST GOT AN *APB* ON A DANGEROUS ESCAPED CON, SO WATCH YOUR STEP.

HEY! THERE'S MY ANSWER!

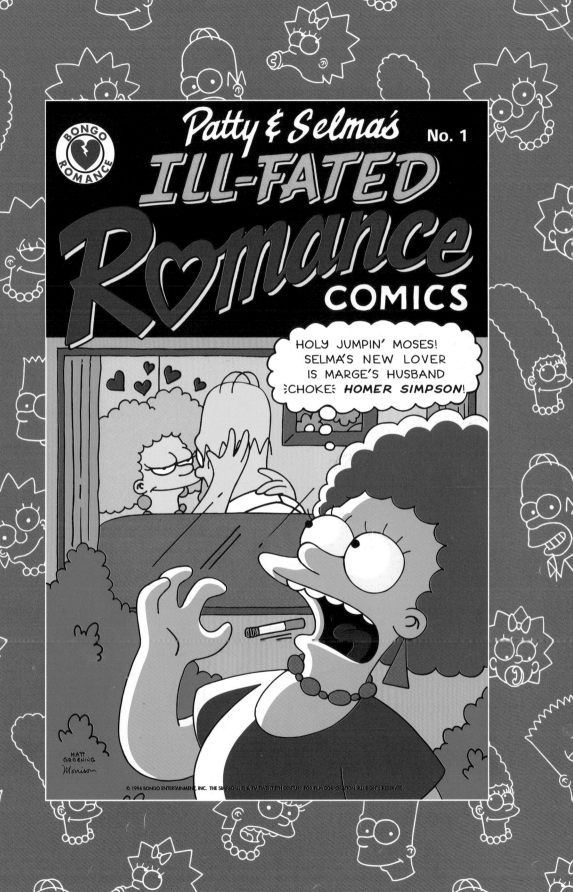

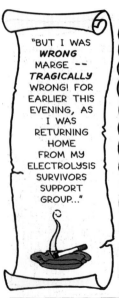

"BUT I WAS *WRONG* MARGE -- *TRAGICALLY* WRONG! FOR EARLIER THIS EVENING, AS I WAS RETURNING HOME FROM MY ELECTROLYSIS SURVIVORS SUPPORT GROUP..."

HOLY JUMPIN' MOSES! IT'S *SELMA*, ABOUT TO *TONGUE-WRESTLE* WITH ⸨GASP⸩ *HOMER!*

...AND THEN I RUSHED RIGHT OVER TO TELL YOU, WHILE *EVERY SLEAZY DETAIL* WAS STILL FRESH IN MY MIND.

YOU GOT ANY MORE MAPLE LOGS?

WELL, I STILL CAN'T BELIEVE IT. HOMER MAY HAVE AN UNBELIEVABLY LONG LIST OF FAULTS, BUT DECEPTION ISN'T ON IT.

OH, *YEAH?* WELL, WHERE IS THE BIG CHOIR BOY NOW?

HE SAID HE WAS GOING TO *MOE'S TAVERN!*

FINE. LET'S CALL HIM.

HELLO, MOE'S TAVERN.

THIS IS MARGE SIMPSON. IS HOMER THERE?

I'M SORRY, MA'AM. I HAVEN'T SEEN YOUR HUSBAND *ALL NIGHT.*

WELL?

HE'S NOT THERE.

HA! ER, I MEAN... I'M SO *SORRY*, DEAR.

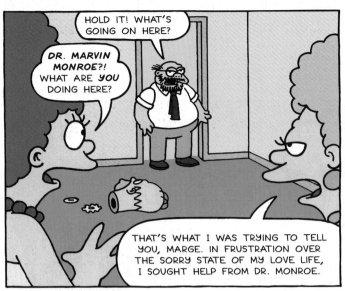

HOLD IT! WHAT'S GOING ON HERE?

DR. MARVIN MONROE?! WHAT ARE YOU DOING HERE?

ALLOW ME TO EXPLAIN, MRS. SIMPSON. AFTER A QUICK CREDIT CHECK, I EXAMINED YOUR SISTER. I SOON DISCOVERED THE ROOT OF HER INCREDIBLY TWISTED MENTAL STATE.

THAT'S WHAT I WAS TRYING TO TELL YOU, MARGE. IN FRUSTRATION OVER THE SORRY STATE OF MY LOVE LIFE, I SOUGHT HELP FROM DR. MONROE.

"SELMAS' JEALOUSY OVER YOUR MARITAL BLISS, COUPLED WITH HER EXTREME CONTEMPT FOR YOUR HUSBAND, HAD CREATED A CONFLICT IN HER SUBCONSCIOUS WHICH CAUSED HER TO SEEK OUT DOOMED RELATIONSHIPS! I SUGGESTED THAT SHE BEGIN A ROMANCE WITH THE OBJECT OF HER JEALOUSY-SLASH-DISGUST AND THEN BREAK IT OFF, THUS FREEING HER TO PURSUE HEALTHIER RELATIONSHIPS."

"HOWEVER, SELMA WAS, ER... RELUCTANT TO ACTUALLY HAVE AN AFFAIR WITH HOMER..."

SPLAK

SO, WITH THE HELP OF THE GOOD FOLKS AT DUFF GARDENS, I CREATED A LIFELIKE AUTO-ANIMATRON® OF YOUR HUSBAND.

SELMA WAS JUST ABOUT TO DUMP THIS FAKE HOMER AND COMPLETE HER THERAPY WHEN YOU INTERRUPTED US.

I'M AFRAID IT MAY TAKE YEARS OF EXPENSIVE TREATMENT TO UNDO THE DAMAGE TO SELMA'S PSYCHE.

"WELL, THAT'S MY SORDID TALE. AND I SWEAR I'LL NEVER DOUBT MY HOMEY'S FIDELITY AGAIN."

SELMA... SELMA...

WHAT THE..?

PACK UP THE WIFE AND KIDS AND HIGH TAIL IT TO PORK FEST '94 SELMA, ALABAMA!

OOH, BABY...

THE END!

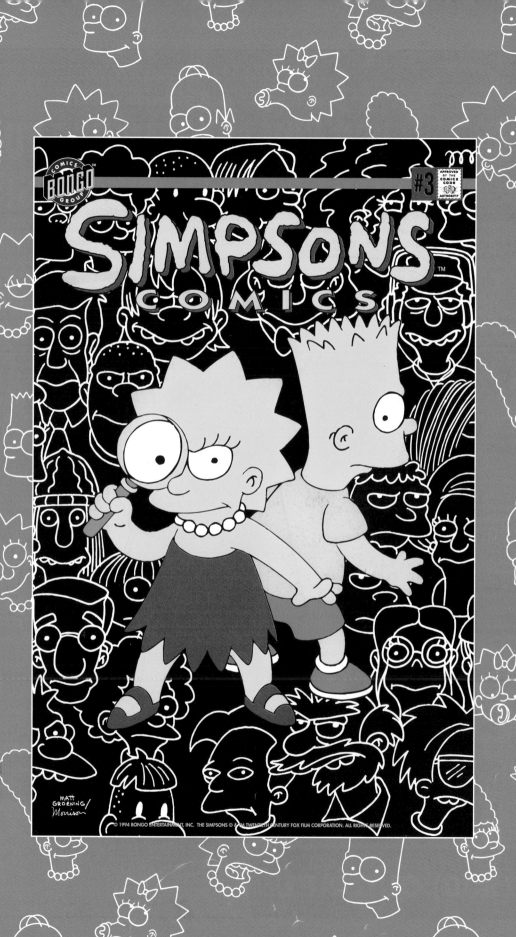

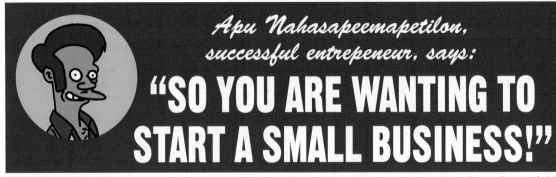

HURRY UP WITH THAT CONCERTINA WIRE, WILLIE -- I WANT OUR MASCOT *SAFE* WHILE I'M AWAY AT THE *PRINCIPALS' CONVENTION!*

-- AND GET THAT *LIGHT* OUT OF MY FACE!

I'LL TELL YE WHERE YE CAN STRING THIS BIT O' WIRE, YE LACE-WEARIN' BOTTLE BABY!

AHEM: I...SUPPOSE YOU ARE THE EXPERT, WILLIE. CARRY ON.

GOOD HEAVENS! HAS EVEN *FAITHFUL WILLIE* TURNED AGAINST ME?

ACH!

MUSTN'T LET MY GUARD DOWN FOR EVEN AN INSTANT. THAT *DISCIPLINARIAN OF THE YEAR AWARD* IS ALMOST WITHIN MY GRASP.

I'D BETTER CHECK IN ON OUR NUMBER ONE TROUBLE SPOT.

HOW GOES OUR LITTLE EXPERIMENT IN *PREEMPTIVE PUNISHMENT*, MS. KRABAPPEL?

I'M NOT SURE WHO IT'S PUNISHING MORE -- BART OR ME.

GOOD, GOOD. CARRY ON.

I WILL NOT RUN A... PRINCIPAL SKINNER IS AWA...

I WILL NOT RUN AMOK WHILE PRINCIPAL SKINNER IS AWAY.

...NOT RUN AMOK WHILE ...AL SKINNER IS AWAY.

...NOT RUN AMOK WHILE ...ICIPA... ...KINNER IS A...

...N... ...UN AMO...

HE'S ACTING STRANGELY -- EVEN FOR *HIM*. I'D BETTER KEEP AN EYE ON HIM.

SHE'S ACTING RATHER PECULIARLY. I'D BETTER KEEP AN EYE ON HER.

SOON...

I'VE WORKED FOR *YEARS* TO BRING ORDER TO THIS SCHOOL, AND IT'S FINALLY GOING TO PAY OFF! IF THERE'S ANY JUSTICE IN THIS WORLD, WHEN THAT AWARD IS HANDED OUT TOMORROW, IT'LL HAVE *SEYMOUR J. SKINNER* INSCRIBED ON IT!

AND YET, ON MY OWN CAMPUS, I'M SURROUNDED BY TREACHERY! WILLIE -- MS. KRABAPPEL -- EVEN THAT TOADYING LITTLE SYCOPHANT *MARTIN PRINCE* SEEMED A TRIFLE INSOLENT TODAY!

ACCUSTOMED AS I AM TO THE LONELINESS OF COMMAND, I STILL LONG FOR A RELIABLE CONFIDANT -- BUT WHO?

WAIT! THERE IS *ONE* MAN --

SPRINGFIELD ELEMENTARY SCHOOL

-- *HONEST ABE LINKLETTER!*

YOU WERE PRINCIPAL DURING THE DARKEST DAYS OF OUR SCHOOL'S HISTORY -- WHEN THE SOUTHERN SUBURBS TRIED TO SECEDE FROM OUR UNITED SCHOOL DISTRICT!

I NEED YOUR GUIDANCE NOW! I --

WHAT AM I *DOING!* I'M TALKING TO AN *INANIMATE OBJECT* --

-- AS IF THIS PAINTING COULD *SPEAK* TO ME!

I'M *ALONE* -- I HAVE NO ONE TO TURN TO --

-- EXCEPT *MOTHER,* OF COURSE!

I GUESS I'VE DONE ALL ONE MAN *CAN* DO. MAY THE PROUD PUMA SPIRIT PROTECT THIS FAIR INSTITUTION DURING MY ABSENCE.

WHAT IN TARNATION WAS *THAT* ABOUT?

I DUNNO, ABE... I THINK OL' SPANKY IS LOSING IT!

HONEST ABE LINKLETTER

SHADY GEORGE WILKINSON

LATER, AS DARKNESS DESCENDS ON SPRINGFIELD...

KREEK

SPRINGFIELD ELEMENTARY SCHOOL

TAK TAK TAK

TAK TAK TAK TAK TAK TAK

IT IS SEVERAL MINUTES PAST THE HOUR AT WHICH *JIMBO, DOLPH,* AND *KEARNY* HABITUALLY ENTER THIS ESTABLISHMENT TO BADGER MY CUSTOMERS!

PERHAPS THEY HAVE ELECTED TO PERFORM THEIR ACTS OF MAYHEM *ELSEWHERE!*

Time for
Duff

:SIGH:
WITHOUT THEIR PATRONAGE, I FEAR I WILL FAIL TO MEET MY *SQUISHEE SALES QUOTA!*

MARTIN, IT'S 7:30. YOU --

SPRINGFIELD PUBLIC LIBRARY

BIOG ALPH

HE'S *NOT HERE!* STRANGE -- THAT LITTLE PRIG *NEVER* LEAVES BEFORE CLOSING TIME! I DO HOPE HE'S NOT *ILL* -- HE'S OUR *ONLY PATRON.*

-- LEAVE YOUR MESSAGE AT THE SOUND OF THE BEEP.

H'LO, EDNA?

EDNA?!

EDNA, IF YOU'RE THERE, PICK UP THE PHONE -- I'M READY FOR A *GOOD TIME!*

FOR A GOOD TIME CALL EDNA K. 555-1776

:BELCH!:

KLIK
SQUEAK

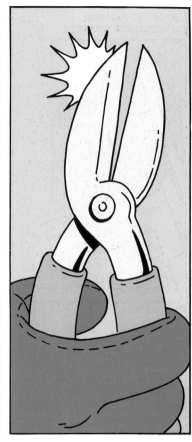

WHERE IS *WILLIE*? HE HA' NE'ER AFORE *MISSED REHEARSAL*!

ACH!

ACH!

HOOT!

SPRINGFIELD
RUM & BAGPI
CORPS

IT'S TIME FOR YOUR ANTIHISTAMINE NOSE DROPS, MILHOUSE --

MILHOUSE?

I'LL BET HE'S SNUCK OVER TO *BART SIMPSON'S HOUSE* AGAIN!

BART, WOULD YOU LIKE SOME *DESSERT*? I MADE *FLOATING ISLAND* --

HMMM... MAYBE HE'S VISITING HIS FRIEND *MILHOUSE*...

THE NEXT MORNING...

WHOA! WHY'S EVERYBODY *OUTSIDE*?! MAYBE SOMEBODY PHONED IN A *BOMB THREAT!*

BUT *I DIDN'T* -- ER, I MEAN, I DON'T KNOW ANYTHING ABOUT IT!

PRINGFIELD ELEMENTARY SCHOOL

YO, MARTIN -- WHAT'S GOING ON, BRAIN-BOY?

IT'S A *DISASTER*, BART! WITH PRINCIPAL SKINNER ABSENT, NO ONE CAME TO OPEN THE BUILDING THIS MORNING! WE'RE *LOCKED OUT!*

WOOHOO! ALL RIIIGHT! SCHOOL IS *CANCELLED!* NOISELAND VIDEO ARCADE, HERE I COME!

CAN THE CELEBRATION, BART -- HERE COMES WILLIE WITH HIS KEYS.

OH, MAN...

BLASTED MULE FELL IN TH' POOL AGAIN -- IT TOOK ME HALF AN HOUR T' HAUL TH' BULLET-RIDDLED CARCASS OUT O' THERE!

NEVER MIND THE COLORFUL ANECDOTES, WILLIE -- JUST OPEN THE DOOR SO WE CAN START CLASS!

WOOHOO! ALL RIIIGHT!

¡GASP!¡

AYE CARUMBA!

THIS IS *TERRIBLE!* SKINNER IS ALMOST AS FIXATED ON THAT PUMA AS HE IS ON HIS *MOTHER!* IF WE DON'T FIND IT BEFORE HE COMES BACK, THERE'LL BE HELL TO PAY!

HE'LL HAVE ME TRANSFERRED TO THE ⟨SHUDDER⟩ *EAST SPRINGFIELD VOCATIONAL TRAINING SCHOOL!*

WELL, IF I HAVE TO GO, I'M NOT TAKING THE FALL *ALONE!*

COME ON, WILLIE! WE'VE GOT *24 HOURS* --

-- *LET'S FIND THAT PUMA!*

ARR...YE COULD NA' FIND...

THAT PITIFUL WAIL -- IT SOUNDS LIKE TH' KEENIN' O' SOME *LOST SOUL!*

L-LOST SOUL? YOU MEAN A *G-GHOST?!*

HMMM... THERE'S SOMETHING STRANGELY *FAMILIAR* ABOUT THAT SOUND...

IT'S COMING FROM OVER THIS WAY!

GOT 'IM CORNERED NOW, DO WE? LET'S SEE HOW THIS DEVIL LIKES A TASTE O' *COLD HIGHLAND STEEL!*

WILLIE! NO! *WAIT!*

OOOOHHH!

ACH! 'TIS ONLY A WEE LADDIE!

MILHOUSE! WHAT ARE YOU DOING IN THERE?!

JIMBO STUFFED ME IN HERE YESTERDAY AFTER SCHOOL!

ACH! YA MILK-DRINKIN' LITTLE PANTYWAIST! I SHOULD HA' SKEWERED YOU WHEN I HAD TH' CHANCE!

SO YOU WERE HERE *ALL NIGHT,* EH, MILHOUSE?

SOMETHING TELLS ME THE TWO OF YOU KNOW WHAT HAPPENED TO THAT *PUMA!* I'M GOING TO GET THE TRUTH OUT OF YOU...

"...IF IT TAKES *ALL AFTERNOON!*"

TALK! *TALK!* TELL ME WHERE THE *PUMA* IS!

HONEST, MS. KRABAPPEL -- WE DON'T KNOW ANYTHING ABOUT IT!

AH, WILLIE -- WHAT HAS YOUR INVESTIGATION TURNED UP?

THERE'S A *BROKEN WINDOW* AT TH' BACK O' TH' BUILDING -- ANY SCURVY WIGHT COULD HA' ENTERED THERE!

SO THE CULPRITS *BROKE IN,* EH?

NAY -- THE WINDOW WAS BROKEN DURIN' THE BRAWL ON *PARENT-TEACHER COOPERATION DAY!* WE HA' NOT HAD THE MONEY FOR A NEW BIT O' GLASS!

I HAVEN'T BEEN ABLE TO GET ANYTHING OUT OF THESE TWO. YOU KNOW WHAT TO DO, WILLIE.

AYE, LASSIE...

...THAT I DO!

YAAAAH!

AN HOUR LATER...

WELL, BOYS -- READY TO *TALK...*

...OR DO I HAVE WILLIE PLAY *"AMAZING GRACE"* AGAIN?

YAAAAH!

NO! STOP! I'LL TELL YOU *EVERYTHING* YOU WANT TO KNOW! THE PLACE WHERE WE HID THE PUMA IS...

SOON...

NO SIGN OF IT! I'M BEGINNIN' T' SUSPECT THOSE LADS DIDNA TELL THE *TRUTH!*

NUCLEAR WASTE TREATMENT CENTER

IN CASE OF E.P.A. RAID, BREAK GLASS

I TRUST THAT WENDELL WAS PROPERLY COURTEOUS WHEN EXTENDING MY INVITATION.

PLEASE SIT DOWN, SIR!

WHY'D YOU DRAG ME HERE, MARTIN?

ALWAYS TO THE POINT, EH, MR. SIMPSON? EGAD, SIR, YOU ARE A REMARKABLE CHARACTER!

I "DRAGGED" YOU HERE TO DISCUSS THE *SPRINGFIELD PUMA!*

WHAT DO *YOU* CARE ABOUT THAT THING? IT'S JUST A *STUPID PLASTER STATUE!*

ON THE CONTRARY, MY FRIEND! MY HISTORICAL RESEARCH HAS REVEALED THE *TRUE NATURE* OF THE PUMA!

IT IS A JEWEL-ENCRUSTED TREASURE, CREATED YEARS AGO BY THE SPRINGFIELD *KNIGHTS OF JEBEDIAH!* IT WAS TO BE SENT TO *CAPITAL CITY* AS A PRIZE IN A *CHARITY RAFFLE*...

...BUT THE PUMA NEVER *REACHED ITS DESTI-NATION!* IT SOMEHOW WOUND UP INSTEAD IN A *SCHOOL CORRIDOR,* IGNORED FOR YEARS, ITS VALUE MASKED BY A COAT OF *GRAY PAINT!*

I WAS DETERMINED TO GAIN POSSESSION OF THE PUMA, REMOVE THE PAINT, AND PRESENT THE STATUE TO THE CITY ON *JEBEDIAH SPRINGFIELD DAY!*

I WOULD HAVE BEEN HAILED AS A CIVIC HERO! IMAGINE THE FUTURE GENERATIONS OF SPRINGFIELDIANS STUDYING MY EXPLOITS IN SCHOOL -- PERHAPS EVEN CELEBRATING *MARTIN PRINCE DAY!*

TO THIS END, I ENLISTED THE AID OF ONE *JIMBO JONES* -- NOT AN IDEAL PARTNER, PERHAPS, BUT HE POSSESSED THE ABILITY TO ACQUIRE THE STATUE BY ANY MEANS NECESSARY!

BUT NOW, JUST AS I AM POISED TO TAKE MY PLACE IN SPRINGFIELD HISTORY, THE PUMA *VANISHES!* PERHAPS JIMBO HAS *DOUBLE-CROSSED ME*...

...BUT I BELIEVE *YOU* KNOW WHERE THE PUMA IS. I SUGGEST YOU *JOIN FORCES* WITH ME. I'LL GIVE YOU *12 HOURS* TO THINK IT OVER --

-- AND YOUR ANSWER HAD BETTER BE *"YES."*

"SHOW OUR VISITOR TO THE DOOR, WENDELL."

SLAM!

AYE CARUMBA! I THINK MARTIN'S GONE OFF THE *DEEP END!* WHAT THE HECK WAS ALL *THAT* ABOUT?!

SOON... THIS THING'S GETTING *TOO DEEP* FOR ME -- I'M GONNA NEED HELP FIGURING IT ALL OUT! FORTUNATELY...

"...I KNOW JUST THE PERSON TO TURN TO FOR SYMPATHY!"

HOME FROM DETENTION SO *SOON*? IT'S HARDLY EVEN *DARK* YET!

I'M IN TROUBLE, LISA.

HEE HEE! *I'LL SAY!* I BET THIS TIME SKINNER'S GOING TO ASK THE JUDGE TO TRY YOU AS AN *ADULT*!

IT'S NOT JUST THAT! LET ME TELL YOU THE REST...

SEVERAL MINUTES LATER... ...SO IF I HELP *MARTIN* FIND THE PUMA, I'LL BE GOING UP AGAINST *JIMBO*! BUT IF THE STATUE *ISN'T FOUND* BY THE TIME *SKINNER* GETS BACK *TOMORROW*, I'LL BE DOING DETENTION TILL I'M *80*!

WELL, BART, SOMEDAY YOU HAVE TO LEARN THAT YOUR *ACTIONS* HAVE *CONSEQUENCES*! PERHAPS THIS IS THE DAY!

LISA, I DIDN'T COME TO YOU TO HEAR ABOUT *LEARNING STUFF*! DON'T YOU *UNDERSTAND*? *I DIDN'T DO IT!*

COME ON, BART -- NOBODY'S LAUGHING AT THAT ONE ANYMORE!

YOU'VE USED UP *EVERY PLOY IN THE BOOK* TO AVOID TAKING RESPONSIBILITY FOR YOURSELF. WHY SHOULD I BELIEVE YOU *NOW*?

LISA, THIS IS YOUR *ONLY BROTHER* TALKING. I'M IN TROUBLE AND I *NEED YOUR HELP*!

PLEASE?

WOW.

RAW, EMOTIONAL *HONESTY* -- THE ONE PLOY YOU *HAVEN'T* OVERUSED!

YOU EVEN SAID THE *MAGIC WORD*!

OKAY, BART! COME ON, THE *GAME IS AFOOT*!

THE FIRST THING WE'VE GOT TO DO IS FIGURE OUT WHO OUR *SUSPECTS* ARE AND START GATHERING INFORMATION ABOUT THEIR ACTIVITIES *LAST NIGHT,* WHEN THE PUMA WAS *STOLEN!*

JIMBO, DOLPH, AND *KEARNY* ALWAYS HANG OUT HERE! SEE WHAT YOU CAN *FIND OUT!*

RIGHT!

'EVENING, APU, MY MAN! GIMME *THE USUAL!*

ONE *JUMBO RED SYRUP SQUISHEE* -- SHAKEN, NOT STIRRED -- COMING RIGHT UP!

AND HERE COME OUR *PRIME SUSPECTS,* RIGHT ON TIME! THIS WILL BE *EASY* -- THESE GUYS WILL NEVER SUSPECT THEY'RE *BEING FOLLOWED!*

"...I JUST HOPE *LISA'S* DOING OKAY."

SKREEE

SPRINGFIELD ELEMENTARY SCHOOL

HERE'S THE *BROKEN WINDOW* BART HEARD ABOUT! I FIGURED THE WHEELS OF THE BUREAUCRACY WOULD GRIND TOO SLOWLY FOR IT TO HAVE BEEN *REPAIRED!*

NOW LET'S SEE IF SKINNER *HIMSELF* HAS ANY EVIDENCE TO SHOW WHO WOULD'VE TAKEN HIS PUMA!

SEYMOUR SKINNER PRINCIPAL

THE NEXT MORNING...

ALL RIGHT, BART -- THIS IS YOUR *LAST CHANCE!* PRINCIPAL SKINNER WILL BE BACK *ANY MINUTE* -- WHAT HAVE YOU DONE WITH THAT *PUMA?!*

I DIDN'T...

WAIT!

SEYMOUR SKINNER PRINCIPAL

BART ISN'T THE *ONLY* SUSPECT HERE, MS. KRABAPPEL.

WELL, WHICH ONE OF THESE HOOLIGANS *WAS* IT, THEN?

IT COULD BE *ANY* OF THEM, OR *NONE* OF THEM. IT *COULD* EVEN HAVE BEEN...

...*YOU*, MS. KRABAPPEL!

WHY, OF ALL THE -- THAT'S *OUTRAGEOUS!*

NO, IT ISN'T. WE'VE BEEN UNABLE TO ESTABLISH WHERE *ANY* OF YOU WERE AT THE TIME OF THE CRIME -- AND *EVERYONE* IN THIS ROOM HAD A *MOTIVE* FOR STEALING THE PUMA!

WHAT MOTIVE?! WHY WOULD *I* DO SUCH A THING?

YOU'VE LONG RESENTED SKINNER'S POSITION OF POWER, WHICH YOU DON'T FEEL HE DESERVES.

AYE! 'TIS *TRUE*!

MANY'S THE DAY I'VE HAD T' LISTEN TO HER *BELLYACHIN'*!

SHE'S THE ONE WHO *DONE IT,* ALL RIGHT!

NOT SO *FAST,* WILLIE! YOU AREN'T EXACTLY *IN LOVE* WITH SKINNER *YOURSELF!* WE'VE *ALL* HEARD *YOU* COMPLAINING ABOUT HIM MAKING YOU POLISH THAT STATUE EVERY DAY!

IT'S TRUE -- DISPOSING OF THE PUMA WOULD HAVE BOTH RID YOU OF THIS UNPLEASANT DUTY *AND* STRUCK A BLOW AGAINST THE MAN WHO MADE YOU PERFORM IT!

ARR...

HA HA!

YOU MAY NOT HAVE THE *LAST* LAUGH, NELSON. AFTER ALL, SKINNER MADE YOU SERVE COUNTLESS DETENTIONS -- SO OF COURSE YOU FEEL A DEEP-SEATED ENMITY TOWARD HIM.

HUH? ENME-*WHAT*?

IT MEANS DISLIKE, HOSTILITY -- EVEN *HATRED,* YOU UNLEARNED OAF!

AS FOR *YOU*, MARTIN, YOUR KNEEJERK RESPECT FOR AUTHORITY WOULD SEEM TO *RULE YOU OUT* AS A SUSPECT -- AT *FIRST GLANCE!* BUT BART HAS TOLD ME ABOUT YOUR LITTLE SCHEME...

...AND ABOUT *YOUR* INVOLVEMENT, JIMBO!

I DON'T KNOW NOTHING -- 'CEPT THAT THIS PUNK *DIDN'T DELIVER!*

AND YOU, MISS HOOVER -- I CHECKED THE SCHOOL DISTRICT'S COMPUTER DATABASE AND LEARNED WHAT WAS IN THAT FILE YOU STOLE! IT WAS *YOUR OWN PERSONNEL RECORD...*

B-BUT...

...INCLUDING THE FACT THAT YOUR BELOVED *GREAT AUNT* WAS *MAULED BY A PUMA* WHEN YOU WERE A CHILD!

PERHAPS YOU SEIZED THE OPPORTUNITY TO DISPOSE OF OUR SCHOOL MASCOT, AN EVER-PRESENT *REMINDER* OF THAT AWFUL TRAGEDY.

UH, LISA -- YOU'VE GONE ALL THE WAY AROUND THE ROOM AND WE *STILL* DON'T KNOW *WHO TOOK THE STATUE!*

MAYBE *YOU* DON'T, BART -- BUT AFTER CAREFULLY ANALYZING ALL THE CLUES, *I* KNOW WHO DID IT...

...AND THAT PERSON IS...

...*PRINCIPAL SKINNER!*

GIVEN HIS OBSESSIVE CONCERN FOR THE WELL-BEING OF HIS BELOVED MASCOT AND HIS MISTRUST OF *ALL* OF YOU, I DEDUCED THAT HE *TOOK THE PUMA WITH HIM* FOR SAFEKEEPING.

WHAT ARE YOU ALL DOING IN MY OFFICE?

ER -- HOW WAS THE *CONFERENCE*, SEYMOUR?

IT WAS A *SHAM* -- A *MOCKERY!* THOSE SMALL-MINDED FOOLS THINK THEY CAN BUY MY SILENT ACQUIESCENCE WITH A "3RD RUNNER-UP" CERTIFICATE, BUT *I* KNOW THAT VOTE WAS *RIGGED* -- AND I WON'T HOLD MY TONGUE *FOREVER!*

HERE, WILLIE -- PUT THIS NOBLE CREATURE BACK ON HIS PEDESTAL WHERE HE BELONGS -- AND BE SURE TO GIVE HIM A *GOOD POLISHING!*

NOW, COME ON, PEOPLE -- LET'S RISE ABOVE MY *PERSONAL CALAMITY!* WE'VE GOT A *SCHOOL* TO RUN HERE!

ACH!

YOU *DID* IT, LISA -- YOU *SAVED* ME!

THAT WAS *GREAT DETECTIVE WORK!*

IT WAS ELEMENTARY, MY DEAR BART -- *SPRINGFIELD ELEMENTARY!* HEE HEE!

HEH, HEH... I DON'T GET IT.

THAT NIGHT...

AT LAST! MY HOUR OF TRIUMPH IS AT HAND! NOW TO REMOVE THE LAYER OF *PAINT* AND UNCOVER THE *TREASURE WHICH LIES BENEATH!*

CHIP! CHIP!

PLASTER! NOTHING BUT *WORTHLESS PLASTER!* AND I WAS SO *SURE*...

MY APOLOGIES, GENTLEMEN -- IT APPEARS MY RESEARCH WAS *IN ERROR!* I TRUST YOU UNDERSTA-AA-*AAA*...

I SHARE YOUR *DISAPPOINTMENT,* GENTLEMEN, BUT I QUESTION YOUR MEANS OF *EXPRESSING IT!*

GENTLEMEN...?

HELLO...?

RATTLE! RATTLE!

THE END!

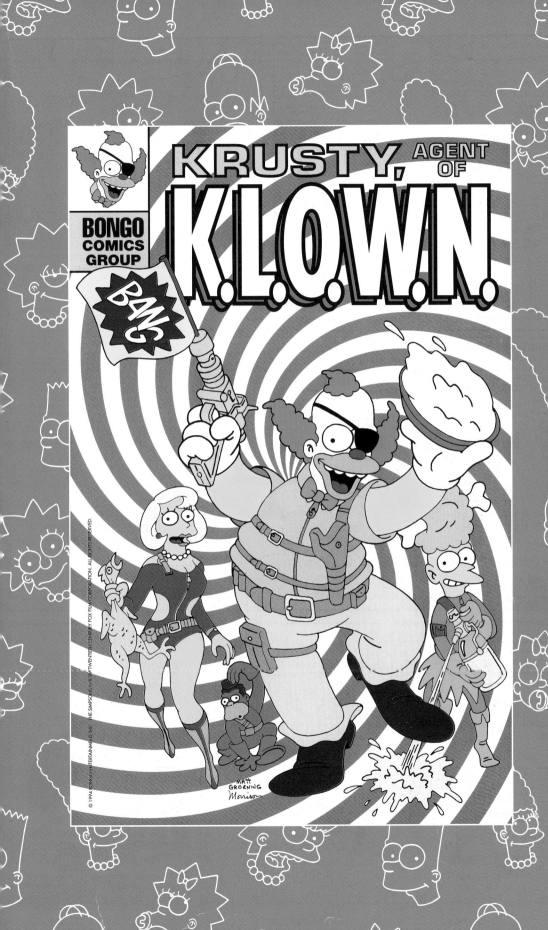

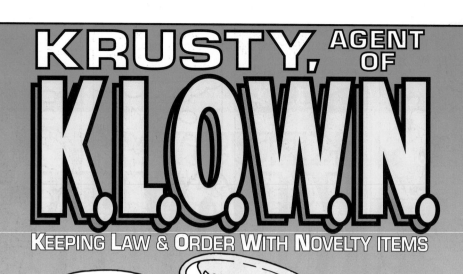

KRUSTY, AGENT OF K.L.O.W.N.

KEEPING LAW & ORDER WITH NOVELTY ITEMS

MR. TEENY -- *NO!* *DON'T TOUCH THAT SWITCH!* IT OPENS THE --

YAAAAAAA!!

A *GROENING* ☆ *CASTELLANETA*
LACUSTA ☆ *VANCE* ☆ *MORRISON*
BAVINGTON ☆ *VANCE* PRODUCTION

**AERIAL CONTROLLED RUDDERLESS
ORDNANCE NODE -- YEAH, MAN!*

⋮WHEW⋮
LUCKY I'M WEARIN'
MY *A.C.R.O.N.Y.M.**
SUIT! WITH THESE
WINGS, I CAN GLIDE
TO SAFETY!

GOOD THING WE WERE RIGHT ABOVE THE *K.L.O.W.N.* TESTING TOWER! I CAN JUST LAND ON THE ROOF!

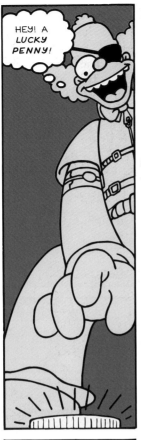

HEY! A *LUCKY PENNY!*

WOOO! A COSMIC ENERGY CREAM PIE CANNON! IF I HADN'T BENT DOWN, *I* WOULDA BEEN CREAMED!

VOONK! VOONK!

SPLAT!

IT'S FIRIN' *TOO FAST* -- CAN'T KEEP UP -- !

VOONK!

OH NO! ONLY HIS *NOSE* REMAINS!

MUST IT COME TO *THIS*?! THE ONE WHO MADE US LAUGH NOW MAKES US *CRY*?!

AHH, QUIT CRYIN' OVER *SPILT CLOWN!*

KRUSTY! YOU'RE *ALIVE!*

OF COURSE! THAT BLOWN-UP HUNK O' JUNK WAS JUST AN *L.M.N.O.P.**!

YOU MEAN THE NEW *ROBOT DOUBLE* DESIGNED TO TAKE YOUR PLACE ON *DANGEROUS MISSIONS*?!

WHAT DANGEROUS MISSIONS? I WAS JUS' GONNA HAVE HIM SUBSTITUTE ON MY *TV SHOW* SO'S I COULD GO TO THE *TRACK!* BELIEVE ME, THE WAY THE AUDIENCE HAS BEEN LATELY, THAT'S *DANGEROUS ENOUGH!*

*LIFE MODEL, *NOT* OFFICIAL PERSON!

LATER, AT K.L.O.W.N. HEADQUARTERS...

I GOT YOUR SIGNAL ON MY **SECRET NOSE PHONE,** CORPORAL PUNISHMENT! WHAT'S THE SITUATION?

YOUR ARCH-ENEMY **GABBO,** THE POWER-MAD VENTRILOQUIST'S DUMMY, AND HIS EVIL ORGANIZATION **W.O.O.D.*** ARE PLOTTING TO **TAKE OVER THE WORLD!** IT'S UP TO **YOU** TO STOP 'EM! THIS COULD BE THE **MOST DANGEROUS THREAT** K.L.O.W.N. HAS EVER FACED!

ER -- DON'T I HAVE SOME **VACATION TIME** COMING UP RIGHT ABOUT NOW?

SIDESHOW MEL HAS DEVELOPED SOME SUPER-SOPHISTICATED NEW WEAPONS FOR YOU TO USE ON THE MISSION. HE'S WAITING FOR YOU OVER IN **ARMAMENTS DIVISION**.

*WORLD ORDER OF DUMMIES

SAY, KRUSTY -- WHAT'S WITH THE **EYEPATCH?**

EYEPATCH?! WHAT TH -- ?!

WELL WHADDYA KNOW?! **NO WONDER** EVERYTHING LOOKED SO **FLAT! MR. TEENY** MUST'VE STUCK IT ON ME WHILE I WAS TAKING A NAP!

SOON, IN THE K.L.O.W.N. ARMAMENTS DIVISION...

HERE'S YOUR FIRST NEW DEVICE. IT'S CALLED A **F.L.O.W.E.R.***!

*FOLIAGE-LIKE OBJECT WITH **EXPLOSIVE RIGGING**

THE OL' **SQUIRTING BOUTONNIERE,** EH? MISS PENNYCANDY **LOVES** THESE THINGS!

SNIFF SNIFF

BAM!

ACTUALLY, THIS ONE **EXPLODES WHEN SNIFFED!**

WOULDN'T IT BE BETTER IF I **THREW IT?!**

THEN, WITH EVERY FIBER OF HIS STOMACH FEELING QUEASY, THE DYNAMIC K.L.O.W.N. RAMROD HURTLES OUT TO SEA...

...THEN, IN THE NEXT INSTANT, OUT OF NOWHERE, A POWERFUL *TRACTOR BEAM,* MADE OF SOMETHING SO SECRET I CAN'T EVEN *THINK IT,* SUCKED ME INTO A HIDDEN AQUA-GELATINOUS OPENING, MUCH LIKE WHEN WHATSISNAME PARTED THE RED SEA IN THAT BIBLE MOVIE!

I WAS HELD CAPTIVE BY *GABBO* IN HIS SECRET ISLAND FORTRESS! THEN YOU, SIDESHOW MEL, MR. TEENY, AND CORPORAL PUNISHMENT BURST IN TO *RESCUE ME* IN THE *KLOWN KAR!* THEN OUR 1000-CLOWN ARMY JUMPED OUT OF THE KLOWN KAR, BUT GABBO'S ROBOT MARIONETTES MASSACRED 'EM!

THEN GABBO'S ORBITING SPACE STATION CRASHED INTO THE ISLAND! *KA-BOOM!* IT WAS SPECTACULAR! WE ESCAPED IN THE KLOWN KAR AND WATCHED THE FORTRESS SINK INTO THE ABYSS! THE OCEAN BUBBLED UP ALL THESE AIR BUBBLES! YOU SHOULDA SEEN IT!

I *DID* SEE IT -- I WAS *THERE,* REMEMBER?

WELL, THAT'S IT! HOW ABOUT IT, GUYS?

THAT WAS THE *WORST* PILOT FOR A *TV SHOW* I'VE *EVER SEEN!*

FORGET THIS *SPY STUFF,* KRUSTY! STICK WITH WHAT YOU *KNOW* -- STAY WITH *COMEDY!*

WHY DIDN'T WE GET TO SEE ALL THAT *ACTION* YOU WERE TALKING ABOUT?

WE RAN OUTTA *MONEY* -- THOSE FREAKIN' *HELICOPTER SHOES* COST A *BUNDLE!* BUT REALLY, WHAT DO YOU THINK OF IT?

WE DIDN'T WANT IT BEFORE --

-- WE DON'T WANT IT *TWICE AS MUCH* NOW!

WE WON'T *EVER* WANT IT!

THEY'RE *GONE* -- AND SO IS MY HOPE FOR A *NEW SHOW!*

VEEP! VEEP!

MY *NOSE PHONE* IS RINGING! HEH HEH...LITTLE DO THEY SUSPECT --

...AND RETURN THAT *NOSE PHONE* TO THE *PROP DEPARTMENT!*

#@$%☆◎!!!

THE END!

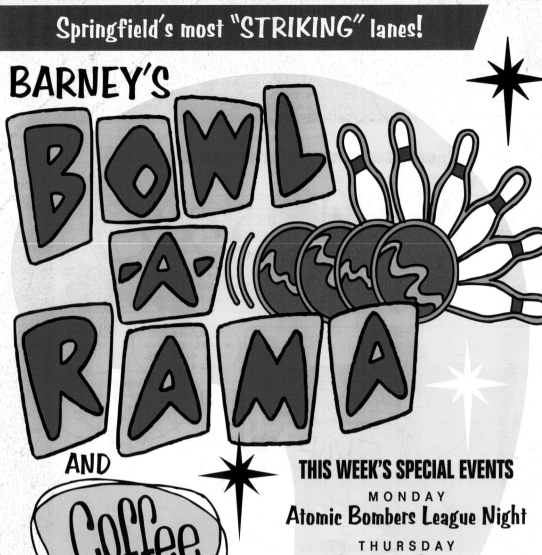

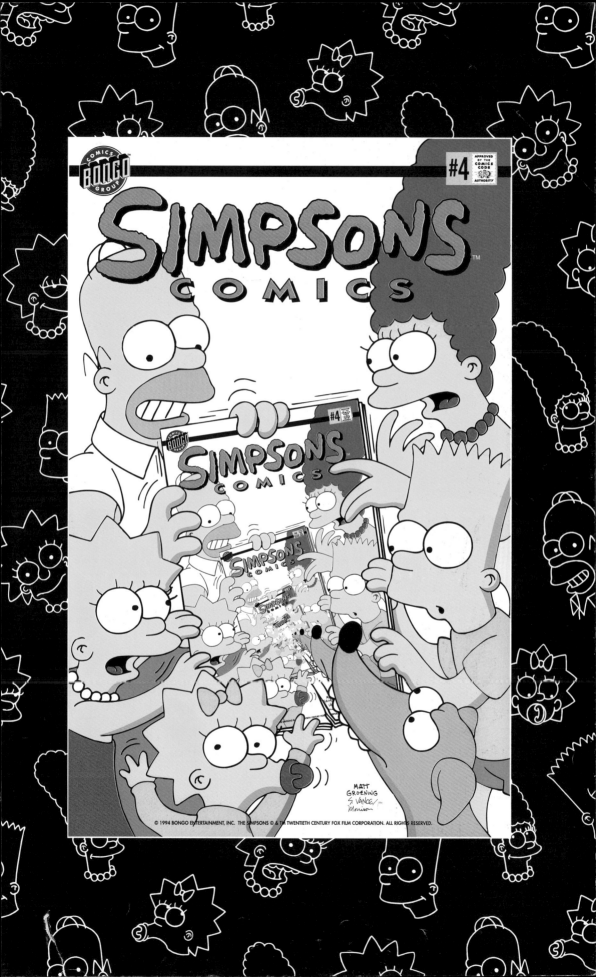

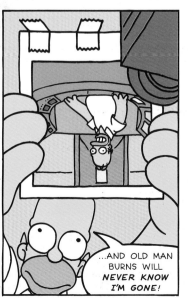

LET'S GO! WE CAN MAKE IT BACK TO WORK IN TIME TO CLOCK OUT!

YAY, ISOTOPES!

WOOHOO! CHEAP BEER!

EMERGENCY EXIT

ELSEWHERE...

HURRY, BART -- BEFORE ANYBODY SEES US!

DON'T WORRY, MAN -- NOBODY'S IN THE HALLS N--

--OW!!

THOOMP

BART -- YOU CLUMSY OAF!

LISA! WHY DON'T YOU WATCH WHERE YOU'RE GOING?!

I JUST SPENT 45 MINUTES COLLATING THESE HANDOUTS ABOUT NEXT WEEK'S JEBEDIAH SPRINGFIELD DAY ARTS & CRAFTS SHOW FOR MISS HOOVER!

NOW I'LL HAVE TO DO THEM ALL OVER AGAIN!

WHAT ARE YOU COMPLAINING ABOUT, MISS TEACHER'S PET? THAT MEANS YOU GET TO SKIP ANOTHER 45 MINUTES OF CLASS! YOU'VE GOT A CUSHY JOB -- YOU SHOULD THANK ME!

YOU THINK I'VE GOT IT EASY?! IT REQUIRES GREAT COMMITMENT TO MAINTAIN THE TRUST OF THE POWERS THAT BE! THEY DON'T GIVE THE KEY TO THE MIMEOGRAPH ROOM TO JUST ANYBODY, YOU KNOW!

MEANWHILE...

AHHHH -- WHAT A BEAUTIFUL DAY! THERE'S NO BETTER WAY TO KILL A FRIDAY AFTERNOON THAN THIS!

GREAT SEATS, TOO!

YEAH -- JUST STEPS AWAY FROM THE *CONCESSION STAND!*

SOON...

--TAPS A SLOW DRIBBLER DOWN THE THIRD BASE LINE--

GLUG GLUG GLUG

DREADNOUGHT O' Duff

MMMMM... FACTORY-SECOND BEER!

--THE PITCH IS *HIGH* AND *TIGHT*, SO THE COUNT IS FULL--

--LIFTS A *LAZY FLY* TO SHALLOW RIGHT--

ZZZ

HUH?! WH-WHUZZAT?!

I SAID, *"CLEAR OUT,"* BUB! THE GAME'S BEEN OVER FOR AN *HOUR!*

YAAAAH!

YOUR PALS *TRIED* T' WAKE YOU BEFORE THEY LEFT, BUT--

OHMIGOSH! IT'S ALMOST 5:00!

I'VE GOT TO GET BACK TO THE POWER PLANT IN TIME TO *CLOCK OUT!*

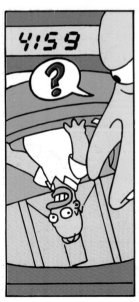

MONDAY MORNING IN THE TEACHERS' LOUNGE AT SPRINGFIELD ELEMENTARY...

HURRY IT UP, PAL!

CAN'T YOU RESTOCK THAT MACHINE ANY FASTER? CLASS STARTS IN *TEN MINUTES* AND I HAVEN'T HAD *BREAKFAST* YET!

DON'T GET YOUR UNDIES IN AN UPROAR, LADY -- I'M ALMOST DONE!

HMMM...THIS STUFF'S USUALLY *FROZEN SOLID!* MUST BE USING SOME NEW *PRESERVATIVES.*

NINE MINUTES LATER...

THERE YOU GO, MA'AM -- SNACK IN GOOD HEALTH!

JERK!

...I BARELY HAVE TIME FOR MY *SAUCY BREAKFAST PATTY-WICH!*

VZZZZZZ

DING!

PLOP!

REMOVE NOW!

SHAKE A LEG, EDNA -- WE GOTTA EAT TOO, Y'KNOW!

MMM...*TANGY!* MAYBE THEY'VE STARTED PUTTING *REAL MEAT* IN THESE BREAKFAST PATTIES!

IT'S MY TURN!

I WAS HERE FIRST!

QUIT SHOVING!

MUNCH MUNCH

BUT TWO HOURS LATER...

YOU BETTER COME T' THE *INFIRMARY,* PRINCIPAL SKINNER! HALF THE FACULTY'S THERE -- IT'S AN *EPIDEMIC!*

CALM YOURSELF, DORIS -- I'M SURE IT'S NOT AS BAD AS ALL THAT. REMEMBER THE TIME YOU THOUGHT THE LITTLE WEIDLER GIRL'S FRECKLES WERE *THE BLACK PLAGUE?*

:SIGH: I MIGHT HAVE KNOWN THERE'D BE A *DOWNSIDE* TO HIRING THE LUNCHROOM LADY AS OUR *NURSE!* THIS TENDENCY TO *EXAGGERATE*--

INFIRMARY

GOOD HEAVENS! :CHOKE:

INFIRMARY

I GUESS WE'LL HAVE TO MAKE THE BEST OF IT. LET'S JUST HOPE THAT FOR ONCE I DON'T HAVE TO CALL IN THE *S.W.A.T. TEAM!*

THE NEXT DAY...

WHAT'S THE MATTER, BART?

OH, MAN -- WE'RE SUPPOSED TO GIVE OUR STUPID *BOOK REPORTS* TODAY, AND I HAVEN'T EVEN *STARTED READING* MY BOOK!

HAVEN'T YOU HEARD? WE'VE GOT A *SUBSTITUTE TEACHER* TODAY!

ALL RIGHT! SUBSTITUTES *NEVER* MAKE US TURN IN OUR ASSIGNMENTS!

?!

SUBSTITUTE TEACHER! COULD IT POSSIBLY BE *MR. BERGSTROM*...? *SIGH*

POOF!

YOU ARE LATE!

BUT CLASS DOESN'T START FOR *FIVE MINUTES* --

WHO DECIDES WHEN CLASS STARTS -- THE *TEACHER*, OR SOME *FALLIBLE MECHANICAL DEVICE*? TAKE YOUR SEAT -- AND NO MORE *BACK TALK!*

NOW GET OUT YOUR NOTEBOOK. OUR FIRST LESSON TODAY WILL BE...

...PENMANSHIP!

MEANWHILE...

...SO, SINCE I DON'T KNOW WHAT MS. KRABAPPEL HAD PLANNED FOR YOU TODAY, I GUESS WE'LL HAVE TO FIND SOME OTHER WAY TO PASS THE TIME. DOES ANY ONE KNOW ANY GOOD *GAMES*?!

MR. SOMERSET

YAAAAY!!

ACTUALLY, MR. SOMERSET, *I* KNOW WHAT WE'RE SUPPOSED TO BE DOING TODAY!

...WE'RE SCHEDULED TO PRESENT OUR *BOOK REPORTS!*

YOU *DIE* AFTER SCHOOL, PUNK!

BOOK REPORTS. HOW...FASCINATING.

OKAY, MARTIN, WHY DON'T YOU GO FIRST?

MUCH LATER...

...BUT AS WE'LL SEE, TOLSTOY HAS ALREADY ESTABLISHED THESE RELATIONSHIPS IN THE FIRST TWO HUNDRED PAGES OF THIS EPIC, THUS--

THANK YOU, MARTIN.

B-BUT I'M NOT DONE YET! I HAVEN'T EVEN MENTIONED THE UNDERLYING --

PUT A SOCK IN IT, KID. NOW LET'S HEAR FROM...

NOT ME. NOT *ME.* *NOT ME.* *NOT ME!*

...BART SIMPSON.

D'OH!

WHOOPS!

PLOP!

HMMM...

WHY NOT?

THE WEEK PASSES...

THURSDAY AFTERNOON...

4:30! THIS IS WORSE THAN *DETENTION!*

HUH? *LISA?!*

WHAT ARE YOU DOING HERE SO LATE?

MISS KELP MADE ME WRITE "I WILL NOT TALK BACK TO MY SUPERIORS" ON THE BLACKBOARD 100 TIMES. YOU'D THINK THAT A *TEACHER* WOULD RECOGNIZE THE WORTHLESSNESS OF SUCH A ROTE EXERCISE. WHAT ARE *YOU* DOING HERE?

MR. SOMERSET MADE ME STAY AFTER STUPID SCHOOL TO HELP HIM MAKE A STUPID BANNER FOR THAT STUPID *ARTS* & STUPID *CRAFTS SHOW* TOMORROW. HE SAID HE WANTED MY "CREATIVE INPUT," WHATEVER *THAT* MEANS!

:SIGH:

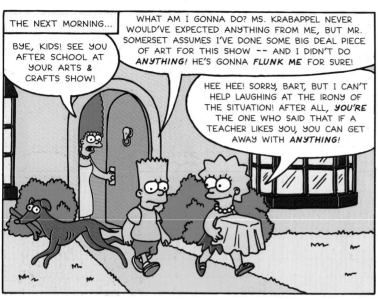

THE NEXT MORNING...

BYE, KIDS! SEE YOU AFTER SCHOOL AT YOUR ARTS & CRAFTS SHOW!

WHAT AM I GONNA DO? MS. KRABAPPEL NEVER WOULD'VE EXPECTED ANYTHING FROM ME, BUT MR. SOMERSET ASSUMES I'VE DONE SOME BIG DEAL PIECE OF ART FOR THIS SHOW -- AND I DIDN'T DO *ANYTHING!* HE'S GONNA *FLUNK ME* FOR SURE!

HEE HEE! SORRY, BART, BUT I CAN'T HELP LAUGHING AT THE IRONY OF THE SITUATION! AFTER ALL, *YOU'RE* THE ONE WHO SAID THAT IF A TEACHER LIKES YOU, YOU CAN GET AWAY WITH *ANYTHING!*

BUT THIS GUY'S *DIFFERENT!* HE'S ALWAYS TALKING ABOUT *SYMBOLS* AND STUFF. I DON'T KNOW WHAT HE MEANS HALF THE TIME -- HEY, MAYBE THAT'S IT! LET'S SEE...

HERE, BOY!

HEY, TEACHER'S PET, WHAT'S WITH THE STICK?

IT'S NOT A STICK, MAN, IT'S...

...IT'S A *SYMBOL!* IT REPRESENTS THE FRAGILE STATE OF OUR NATURAL ENVIRONMENT...

???

I DON'T GET IT, MARGE -- IT STILL LOOKS LIKE A STICK.

...OR MAYBE IT REPRESENTS THE, UH, TRAGIC LONELINESS OF THE HUMAN CONDITION, OR...

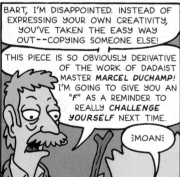

BART, I'M DISAPPOINTED. INSTEAD OF EXPRESSING YOUR OWN CREATIVITY, YOU'VE TAKEN THE EASY WAY OUT--COPYING SOMEONE ELSE!

THIS PIECE IS SO OBVIOUSLY DERIVATIVE OF THE WORK OF DADAIST MASTER *MARCEL DUCHAMP!* I'M GOING TO GIVE YOU AN "F" AS A REMINDER TO REALLY *CHALLENGE YOURSELF* NEXT TIME.

:MOAN:

MEANWHILE...

THIS SAND CASTING REPRESENTS THE *MANY RACES AND CULTURES* WHO HAVE *JOINED HANDS* TO MAKE OUR CITY WHAT IT IS TODAY.

WHISK!

EXCELLENT, LISA--

-- I WHOLEHEARTEDLY AGREE! THE *EVIL FORCES* OF POLITICALLY CORRECT *MULTI-CULTURALISM* ARE TO BLAME FOR THE DISGRACEFUL CONDITION OF OUR CITY! YOUR FINE PIECE OF RIGHT-THINKING SOCIAL CRITICISM DESERVES AN "A"!

BUT *THAT'S* NOT WHAT I *MEANT* --

MONDAY MORNING...

HEY, BART! THE NEW SERIES OF BASEBALL CARDS IS OUT! AND I ONLY HAD TO BUY **58 PACKS** BEFORE I FOUND THIS ONE!

LEMME SEE, MAN.

LOOK -- IT'S THE PHOTO OF **WILLY DIPKIN** THEY TOOK THE DAY WE WERE THERE! HE'S MAKING THE CARD COMPANY **TAKE IT OFF THE MARKET** BECAUSE SOMEBODY **WROTE** ON THE HANDLE OF HIS **BAT!**

THAT MAKES THIS CARD AN **ULTRA-RARE COLLECTOR'S ITEM!** IT'LL BE WORTH A **FORTUNE!**

HAHA! HAHA! HEH HE HO!

GOOD MORNING, CLASS!

GULP!

DID YOU MISS ME?

YAAAAAH!!

AND SO... AHH! MISS HOOVER'S BACK, AND WITH HER COME THE SMALL DELIGHTS OF THE RETURN TO NORMALCY! THE SHINY KEY TO THE MIMEOGRAPH ROOM -- THE FRESHLY SMUDGED COPIES OF TOMORROW'S HANDOUTS --

-- AND THE SIGHT OF **BART** BACK IN HIS **NATURAL HABITAT!**

HEE HEE!

I WILL NOT MANIPULATE THE
I WILL NOT MANIPULATE THE
I WILL NOT MANIPULATE THE
I WILL NOT MANIPULATE THE

THE END!

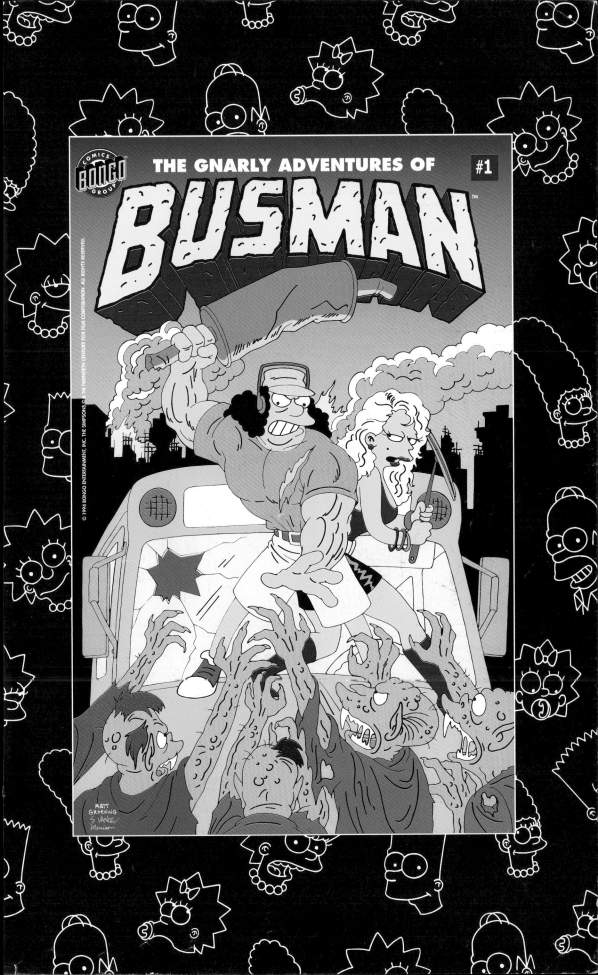

THE DESERT. A ROAD STRETCHES ACROSS THIS BARREN WASTELAND, FLAT AND STRAIGHT LIKE THE NECK OF A REALLY, REALLY HUGE GUITAR, ONLY IT'S MADE OF CONCRETE AND HAS A YELLOW LINE DOWN THE MIDDLE OF IT.

FEW DARE TRAVEL HERE, FOR, IN THE YEARS SINCE THE *NUCLEAR WAR*, THIS HAS BECOME THE DOMAIN OF THE *MUTANT VAMPIRES*, THESE REALLY GNARLY DUDES WITH GREAT BIG POINTY TEETH.

IT IS A *HARD WORLD* -- A *LONELY WORLD* -- A *DANGEROUS WORLD.*

NOWHERESVILLE

ALL KINDS OF *SCARY STUFF* LURKS AROUND EVERY CORNER.

SPLAT

BUT THIS IS *MY* WORLD.

I AM...

BUSMAN

STEVE VANCE
SCRIPT, LAYOUTS

BILL MORRISON
PENCILS

TIM BAVINGTON
INKS

CINDY VANCE
COLORS

MATT GROENING
FELLOW TRAVELLER

FOR LOTSA MY PASSENGERS, MY BUS IS THEIR ONLY LINK TO CIVIL-IZATION -- THE LAST THREAD IN THE TATTERED FABRIC OF SOCIETY.

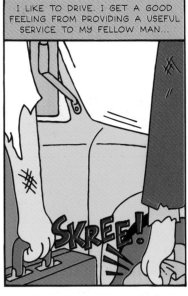

I LIKE TO DRIVE. I GET A GOOD FEELING FROM PROVIDING A USEFUL SERVICE TO MY FELLOW MAN...

SKREE!

...BUT MAINLY I DO IT 'CUZ IT'S SO *COOL!*

WHERE TO, DUDES?

TO *THE CITY,* MY GOOD MAN! I TRUST *THIS* WILL BE ADEQUATE COMPENSATION!

IT'S A *START,* BUT I CAN'T *EAT* MONEY, Y'KNOW!

VERY WELL -- SHOW HIM *WHAT ELSE* WE HAVE TO OFFER!

WHOA! WHY DIDN'T YOU *SAY* SO? HOP IN, MAN!

JIMI HENDRIX THE FEEDBACK SESSIONS

BIRTH of the WAH WAH PEDAL VOL. 6

THE NEW DUDES MADE THEIR WAY TO THE BACK OF THE BUS, JOINING THE OTHER PASSENGERS:

THE FLOOZY, WHO GOT RUN OUT OF TOWN AT THE LAST STOP.

THE LUSH, WHO DOESN'T REMEMBER WHERE HE'S GOING.

THE MISSIONARY LADY, WHO IS JOINING HER HUSBAND TO PREACH TO THE HEATHENS IN THE CITY.

THE BOUNTY HUNTER, WHO SAYS HE'S GOT "BUSINESS" IN THE CITY.

LATE IN THE AFTERNOON, I PULLED INTO THE TRADING POST. IT'S THE ONLY PLACE THAT'S STILL OPEN FOR THE NEXT 500 MILES -- AND MAN, ARE THEIR PRICES HIGH!

I WAS STOCKING UP ON VITAL SUPPLIES WHEN...

HELLO THERE...

...IS THAT *YOUR BUS* OUTSIDE?

I BOUGHT HER A BREW AND SHE TOLD ME HER STORY...

WHERE YOU HEADED?

ANYWHERE BUT HERE. I GOT THIS FAR, THEN MY MONEY RAN OUT.

THE MANAGER AT THE LAST PLACE I WORKED GOT FRESH, SO I BROKE THIS OVER HIS HEAD!

ALL *RIIIGHT!* SHAME ABOUT YOUR GUITAR, THOUGH.

YEAH! NO AXE, NO GIG. NO GIG, NO MONEY!

HEY, NO PROBLEMO! FELLOW MUSICIANS *RIDE FREE!* MAYBE YOU CAN GET YOUR GUITAR FIXED IN THE CITY!

THANKS!

WE PULLED OUT AT DUSK. THE VAMPIRES WOULD BE OUT SOON, SEARCHING FOR *FRESH BLOOD!*

AS I WATCHED THE SUNSET IN THE REARVIEW MIRROR, I FIGURED WE WERE SAFE AS LONG AS WE KEPT MOVING.

BUT I FORGOT *ONE THING...*

...YOU CAN'T SEE VAMPIRES IN THE REARVIEW MIRROR!

KRASH

THE FIRST GUY HAD A GLASS JAW.

ANOTHER ONE TRIED TO SNEAK IN THE SIDE DOOR, BUT I TALKED HIM OUT OF IT.

MEANWHILE, THIS OTHER DUDE ATTACKED THE PASSENGERS. I COULDN'T GET THERE IN TIME...

...BUT SOMETIMES IT HELPS TO HAVE A *MISSIONARY* ON BOARD!

I KICKED HIM OUT, THEN I FIGURED I'D BETTER GET BACK TO DRIVING THE BUS.

SMASH

BUT THE LAST GUY WAS ONE TOUGH DUDE! THINGS WERE GETTING PRETTY HAIRY WHEN...

HANG ON, BUSMAN!

YAAAARGH!

SKLUTCH!

THE REST OF THE NIGHT WAS *QUIET* -- EXCEPT THAT BOUNTY HUNTER DUDE REALLY *SNORED*.

WE REACHED THE CITY AT DAWN.

ENTERING GARLICVILLE VAMPIRE-FREE ...NATURALLY!

'CUZ WE HAD ALL, LIKE, BONDED DURING OUR LIFE-OR-DEATH STRUGGLE, PARTING WAS KINDA BITTERSWEET...

LATER, DUDES!

NO TIP FOR THAT RUFFIAN, SMITHERS!

NO, SIR!

SO...WHERE'RE YOU GONNA GO NOW?

WELL... HOW 'BOUT WHEREVER *YOU'RE* GOING?

COOL!

WHAT'S YOUR *NAME*, ANYWAY?

YOU CAN CALL ME... *BUSBABE!*

LEAVING GARLICVILLE VAMPIRES NEXT 400 MILES

THE END!